PRESERVATION:
TOWARD AN ETHIC
IN THE 1980s

D0103130

THE PRESERVATION PRESS
National Trust for Historic Preservation
1785 Massachusetts Avenue, N.W.
Washington, D.C. 20036

The National Trust for Historic Preservation, chartered by Congress in 1949, is the only private, nonprofit organization with the responsibility to encourage public participation in the preservation of sites, buildings and objects significant in American history and culture. Support is provided by membership dues, endowment funds and contributions and by matching grants from federal agencies, including the U.S. Department of the Interior, Heritage Conservation and Recreation Service, under provisions of the National Historic Preservation Act of 1966.

Library of Congress Cataloging in Publication Data

Preservation: Toward an Ethic in the 1980s

Recommended goals from a national conference, Williamsburg, Va., March 1979, sponsored by the National Trust for Historic Preservation, and papers from the future directions symposia, National Trust for Historic Preservation annual meeting, Chicago, October 1978.

    1. Architecture—United States—Conservation and restoration—Addresses, essays, lectures. 2. Historical buildings—United States—Conservation and restoration—Addresses, essays, lectures. I. National Trust for Historic Preservation in the United States.

NA106.P73   363.6'9'0973   80-17564
ISBN 0-89133-079-8

Book Design by Tom Engeman

PRESERVATION: TOWARD AN ETHIC IN THE 1980s

NATIONAL TRUST FOR HISTORIC PRESERVATION

Recommended goals from a National Preservation Conference,
Williamsburg, Va., March 1979, sponsored by
the National Trust for Historic Preservation,
and papers from the Future Directions Symposia,
National Trust for Historic Preservation
annual meeting, Chicago, October 1978

The Williamsburg conference and this publication
were made possible through a grant from
the Rockefeller Brothers Fund

THE PRESERVATION PRESS

CONTENTS

FOREWORD

Thirteen years have passed since the last national gathering in Williamsburg, Va., to consider the future of the American preservation movement. There was a shared sense of optimism at the 1967 meeting generated by the wealth of new federal preservation legislation signed into law the year before. With this government action, private historic preservation programs began changing significantly in scope and scale. The intervening 13 years saw a most dramatic change in the American preservation experience.

Preservation: Toward an Ethic in the 1980s is the result of a suggestion made at a 1977 meeting of the National Trust for Historic Preservation Board of Trustees' Committee on Long Range Plans. Robert R. Garvey, Jr., Frederick C. Williamson and William J. Murtagh were guests of the committee and, recognizing preservation's continuing evolution, made the suggestion that it was time to pause, take stock of where we were and chart where we might wish to go in the coming decade. The Board of Trustees enthusiastically endorsed the recommendation.

The National Trust 1978 annual meeting in Chicago was the platform chosen to begin this look into the future. The well-attended and well-received Future Directions Symposia and the special insight tours at that meeting clearly indicated that the preservation constituency was eager, opinionated and optimistic about the future.

The National Trust is grateful for the generous support of the Rockefeller Brothers Fund, which enabled the Trust to sponsor two subsequent steps: the convening of a cross-section of the preservation movement in Williamsburg, Va., in March 1979 to delineate more specifically the future of the private sector, and the publication of this book based on that conference.

The years prior to 1979 were not without efforts to consider the future but they were largely organized by, and largely focused on, future public policy and programs. Such efforts included the January 1976 study report to Sen. Henry M. Jackson of Washington by the Advisory Council on Historic Preservation; the 1976 American-produced Bicentennial issue of *Monumentum* for the International Council on Monuments and Sites; the Department of the Interior's 1977 National Heritage Program Task Force and President Carter's 1978 Congressional Urban Policy Message.

Thus, it is most timely that this book be published to enable a larger audience to focus on the private sector's future in American preservation efforts. Recognizing the enormous impact of federal policy on historic preservation in the past 13 years, we must be mindful of such recent developments as:

1. The congressional committees that have been engaged in laying the groundwork for the first oversight hearings of the nation's preservation program since 1966.

2. The several key pieces of historic preservation legislation that are up for reauthorization—the funding for the National Historic Preservation Fund and the historic preservation provisions of the Tax Reform Act of 1976.

3. The proposed legislation for the National Heritage Program.

4. A developing conflict at the state and local levels between rising preservation interests and efforts to reduce local tax income.

What role, then, does America's private sector wish to play in preservation in the coming decade? We have become specialized and diversified, and we have begun to have an impact far more significant than ever before. Increasing success, an expanded public acceptance and an expanded public presence have brought new problems and challenges.

The National Trust was pleased to create and sponsor this most recent Williamsburg conference to explore the private sector's future. Our nation's public and private preservation sectors are constituted of an amazing diversity of individuals and organizations from the local to the international. Those invited to the conference represented some elements of that mosaic. We were not there to discuss the private sector's future in the context of any one organization.

Instead, a platform was created and an opportunity offered whereby the accumulated experiences of those in attendance served as a base, from which we could rise above our own segmented interests and delineate our findings and make recommendations for the future. The Williamsburg conference presented us with an opportunity to identify, discuss and clarify those issues and their related activities that will enable the private sector to move individually and collectively even more forcefully in spreading and strengthening a national preservation ethic in the 1980s. This book brings together the intense thought of that conference.

Recently, newscasts were full of exciting astronomical revelations coming from the Voyager spacecraft and this century's last solar eclipse in North America. It reminded me that my predecessor, Gordon Gray, in his speech entitled "Decade of Decision" to the National Trust 1966 annual meeting turned to astrology to question whether the "moon was right" for preservation. His interpretation of the horoscope indicated that it was right in 1947 when a small band of professionals, propelled by circumstances and perception, took steps to make preservation initiatives a matter of national concern. Further, he believed that it was again right in 1966 when clearer circumstances and a broader and deeper perception impelled people to make preservation not only of national concern but of national action.

While not professing any great astrological powers, I would venture to say that the moon is once again right. The astrological calendar indicates that it is time to move historic preservation from a movement of enthusiastic proponents to a national ethic.

Carlisle H. Humelsine, chairman
Board of Trustees
National Trust for Historic Preservation

PART 1:
RECOMMENDED GOALS

INTRODUCTION

The private preservation movement has come a long way since 1967. We now have the opportunity to rethink, refine and improve on the efforts of the past 13 years. The 1979 National Preservation Conference was a beginning step in this direction. The findings of that conference presented in this section are intended to stimulate discussion and encourage action by individuals and institutions in the private sector as they seek to plan an agenda for the 1980s, an agenda that the National Trust hopes will result in a stronger preservation ethic.

For more than 30 years, the National Trust has given national leadership, impetus and support to private preservation efforts throughout the United States. Today, more than 155,000 individuals, 1,600 organizations, 180 corporations and 100 foundations make up the National Trust membership. Five years ago, the National Trust membership was 98,000. At the time of the preservation conference in 1967, the membership was only 12,000. This rapid increase is a further indication of the growing interest nationwide in historic preservation and of the leadership role of the National Trust.

Planning of Conference

The conference planning committee, appointed in 1977 by the chairman of the National Trust Board of Trustees, met regularly for the next two years to oversee the conceptualization, planning and conduct of both the Chicago and Williamsburg conference components. The committee members were:

Chairman: Robertson E. Collins, Medford, Ore.*
Members: Helen Abell, Louisville, Ky.*
            Charles M. Black, Honolulu, Hawaii*
            Alan S. Boyd, Washington, D.C.*
            Richard W. Freeman, Jr., New Orleans, La.*
            Margot Gayle, New York, N.Y.
            Robert C. Giebner, Tucson, Ariz.*
            Mrs. William M. Lamont, Aberdeen, N.D.*
            Chester H. Liebs, Burlington, Vt.
            Robert E. Stipe, Chapel Hill, N.C.*
            Carl B. Westmoreland, Cincinnati, Ohio*
            Member, Board of Trustees, National Trust

In preparation for the national conference, each of five selected subject areas (funding; objectives, roles and organizational structure; communications; standards, practices
and professionalism; and future directions) was discussed
at the National Trust 1978 annual meeting in Chicago. The
committee's review of these sessions resulted in the addition of separate topics on education, information resources
and terminology, legislation and preservation as an avocation and vocation to be considered during the national conference in March 1979. Distinguished guests also were invited to contribute their perspectives and to prompt discussion
among those present. Their remarks make up Part 2 of this
book.

Participants

One hundred sixteen people were invited to participate from
throughout the United States (see page 239). Their names
came from a categorized listing of private and public constituencies within the preservation movement proposed by
the committee. Names suggested by the committee, National Trust staff and others were indexed against this categorized constituent list, and efforts were made to assure
the broadest possible representation. The committee also
considered geographic, age, sex, ethnic and socioeconomic
factors in an attempt to achieve balance. As an "ice breaker"
those invited were encouraged to complete a specially designed poster entitled "Personal Preservation Profile"; these
were displayed at the opening reception of the conference.

Conference Process

To assist in planning the conference, the committee re-
tained Design Communication Collaborative of Washington, D.C. The conference process was directed at achieving
maximum utilization of the group's collective experience
in the time available and to produce draft reports by the end
of the conference. In advance of the conference, participants
were sent a notebook containing the papers presented at
the 1978 Chicago Future Directions Symposia and the issue
papers prepared by National Trust staff, and they were encouraged to prepare and bring additional materials appropriate to the conference topics.

Participants were assigned to one of eight working groups

on the following topics: objectives, roles and organizational structure; standards and practices; preservation: avocation and vocation; education; communications; information resources and terminology; funding; and legislation. Reassignments were made later based on expressed preferences. Members of the conference planning committee and other participants served as group moderators to direct the work. National Trust staff served as recorders as information was developed. It will be obvious to the reader that not all subjects could be treated as fully as others in the time available in Williamsburg.

The groups met in a series of issue identification and problem-solving sessions each day, at the end of which representatives presented the findings to the entire group for discussion. Draft findings were prepared and reproduced during the evening to share with all participants the following morning. The plenary sessions and guest speakers' presentations were recorded on videotape.

Editorial Process

The findings of each group were circulated in May to each individual who participated in that group for review and comment. A brochure highlighting the conference findings was prepared for distribution in conjunction with National Trust President James Biddle's annual report to the membership at the October 1979 annual meeting in San Francisco.

An editorial review committee consisting of each of the working group moderators, recorders and at least one designated participant convened in January 1980 to review the edited findings based on the comments received from participants. The final report of the conference findings, organized into nine subject areas, presents their editorial review.

It should be noted that the goals represent a consensus viewpoint of the working group participants. However, the suggested enabling steps or means of implementation did not in all instances reflect a unanimous viewpoint.

Findings

The outline format used in presenting the conference findings consists of four elements:

INTRODUCTION: a brief general overview statement of the working groups' major concerns with their subject.

GOAL: the specific recommendations towards which the private sector should be working in the 1980s.

ENABLING STEPS: a range of general activities to be undertaken in furtherance of achieving a specific goal.

MEANS OF IMPLEMENTATION: a range of suggested ways of implementing activities.

It was understood by all participants that this material would represent an agenda for a period of years and that the governing bodies and administrations of the affected agencies and organizations would have to review and consider these findings.

The members of the conference planning committee, especially the chairman, and the editorial review committee merit a special acknowledgment for the many hours of work in this effort. The National Trust is especially appreciative of the assistance of the staff of the Colonial Williamsburg Foundation in facilitating many aspects of the March 1979 conference.

Preservation is most often achieved at the local level by enthusiastic, dedicated private citizens and organizations, with increasing support and encouragement from public officials and agencies. The 1979 National Preservation Conference began a process that can be of great benefit to all those individuals and organizations interested in preserving the best of America's heritage in the decade of the 1980s and beyond.

Russell V. Keune, AIA
Conference Moderator
Senior Vice President, Preservation Services
National Trust for Historic Preservation

OBJECTIVES, ROLES AND ORGANIZATIONAL STRUCTURE

In recent years historic preservation has become multifaceted. As it has broadened its areas of activity, the movement has become increasingly prone to conflicts and confusion about direction and purpose. In the 1980s the preservation movement should focus its priorities and develop a better understanding of the limits of its resources. The preservation movement can control some activities; it can influence other actions; and it can cooperate with and build alliances with related organizations.

GOAL: CULTURAL ENVIRONMENT

To identify, evaluate, protect and interpret essential elements of the cultural environment, including landmarks, cultural conservation districts, archeological sites and museums.

ENABLING STEP

Developing and promoting a broad definition of the cultural environment with reaffirmation of the value of local significance.

MEANS OF IMPLEMENTATION
Historic Districts

Recognize the conceptual limitations of the current terminology, "historic district," and replace it with "cultural conservation district."

Redefine the approach to establishing district boundaries to include recognition of the districts' natural tendency toward expansion.

Maintain diversity by encompassing broad design criteria for both old and new structures.

Develop protection strategies that are consonant with utilization and vitality.

Streetscapes

Recognize streetscapes as a unifying element in communities.

15

Use streetscapes as a measure of design quality in new design as well as rehabilitation.

Articulate the elements of streetscapes in order to educate community residents.

Rural Areas

Develop definitions for rural conservation districts.

Define rural preservation and planning in the context of the full cultural landscape.

Develop criteria for new construction in rural areas.

Landmarks

Utilize landmarks to the broadest extent, in both traditional and new ways.

Maintain appropriate surroundings for landmarks.

Use selected landmarks as models of preservation.

Promote the highest professional standards in the preservation of landmarks.

Archeological Sites

Identify prehistoric and historic archeological sites.

Protect and conserve prehistoric and historic archeological sites, excavating only if scientifically justified.

Museums

Expand the heritage represented by museums.

Encourage greater vitality and creativity of interpretation for historical museums.

Encourage the development of standards and techniques to conserve artifacts integral to this interpretation.

GOAL: COMMUNITY REVITALIZATION EFFORTS

To assist, catalyze and work as a partner in community enhancement and revitalization efforts in neighborhoods, business centers, small towns and rural areas.

ENABLING STEP

Creating partnerships that will protect the integrity of neighborhood cohesion, utilizing economic, social, organizational, political and technical strategies to improve community livability.

MEANS OF IMPLEMENTATION
Technical Assistance (Buildings and Codes)

Provide necessary technical resources to preserve housing and commercial stock.

Encourage sensitive home maintenance and provide necessary technical resources and legal guidelines when public financing is involved.

Create mechanisms for interpretation and flexibility in application of health, safety, building and fire codes.

Develop design solutions for handicapped access that cause minimal damage to the historic fabric of buildings, and inform owners, organizations and professions of these solutions.

Technical Assistance (Organizational)

Encourage the development of proper management skills, financial bases and maintenance techniques to strengthen local community organizations.

Catalyze the formation of voluntary neighborhood associations that will be responsive to local community needs while being supportive of the partnership process.

Economic-Investment

Implement strategies of private reinvestment, particularly through the use of revolving funds, joint banking ventures and private-public partnership financial packaging.

Utilize national affiliations and forums to inform banking, real estate, insurance and business development institutions of the financial benefits of preservation.

Develop economic models and monitoring techniques to prevent "overheating" of neighborhood property values that might cause displacement problems.

Work closely with community groups, businesses and public agencies to encourage the sensitive development of tourism.

Provide technical resources for tour programs to demonstrate the educational benefit of historic preservation.

Monitor the potential impact of tourism on the rights of community privacy and on property values.

Develop strategies to minimize the negative consequences of tourism.

Demonstrate that preservation creates jobs.

Encourage skill development for the implementation of preservation and rehabilitation projects.

Home Ownership

Encourage home ownership to stabilize neighborhoods socially and economically.

Government Relations

Assist in development of neighborhood policy at national, state and local levels.

Assure that the designation of historic districts reinforces neighborhood and community plans and aspirations.

Provide mechanisms to involve the public, quasi-public, private, volunteer, labor and educational sectors in the development of policies and programs for community revitalization.

Educate, provide information and lobby for changes in laws, policies and programs to encourage the integration of preservation goals with other major national, state and local agendas.

GOAL: COALITIONS

To build coalitions and alliances at the national, state and local levels with related institutions whose actions affect preservation.

ENABLING STEPS

Facilitating the creation of long-term coalitions among the various groups concerned with quality in the built environment (e.g., preservationists, neighborhood conservationists, arts advocates, environmentalists) at the state and local levels.

Facilitating the development of long-term mechanisms to foster understanding and cooperation among the various groups whose actions or policies affect quality of life in the built environment (e.g., a work group of developers, public funding agencies, elected officials, bankers, regulators, designers, etc.).

Undertaking with these groups joint programs that will demonstrate and encourage sensitivity to preservation concerns.

MEANS OF IMPLEMENTATION

Develop demonstration projects that reflect the coalition's interest and that recognize the multifaceted arena of preservation.

APPROPRIATE STRUCTURE

The question of an appropriate organizational structure for the preservation movement was implicit but unsolved in the deliberations at Williamsburg. The failure to arrive at recommendations in this area reflects the pluralistic nature of the private sector and its fundamentally nonhierarchic character. It may be reasonable to assume that the vitality of the preservation movement depends on its openness to a variety of organizing principles and frameworks at local, state and national levels. At the same time the 1980s will challenge the preservation movement with increasing competition for resources and with the need to present a unified voice on goals and objectives. The issue papers included in this volume (Part 4) raise many of the central questions about organizational structure.

OBJECTIVES, ROLES AND ORGANIZATIONAL STRUCTURE
Working Group

Robert Berner	Mary C. Means, *Moderator, Recorder***
Minnette C. Bickel	Louise McAllister Merritt
Tersh Boasberg	Michael Middleton
William A.V. Cecil	William J. Murtagh
Carol Clark	Christopher Owens
Susan Dewitt	Frank H. Spink, Jr.
Frances Edmunds	Jan Thorman
Robert R. Garvey, Jr.	Beatrice Utley
William B. Hart, Jr.*	Carl B. Westmoreland, *Moderator*
J. Myrick Howard	Douglas P. Wheeler
Robert P. Lynch, *Recorder**	
Charles R. McGimsey III	**Member, Editorial Review Committee*

19

STANDARDS AND PRACTICES

Better standards and improved practices are essential for assuring quality in the preservation of America's cultural resources. Both standards and practices should be set and carried out at the highest levels of excellence. A standard is defined as a rule established by a recognized authority and a practice as the actual performance of actions governed by a rule. The U.S. Department of the Interior's Heritage Conservation and Recreation Service, Advisory Council on Historic Preservation, National Trust and other national public and private organizations and interests should collaborate in creating and periodically evaluating interrelated standards and monitoring preservation practices so that these efforts are conducted with quality, efficiency and harmony.

GOAL: INTEGRATED SYSTEM

To establish an integrated system for developing, promulgating and evaluating preservation standards involving governmental, institutional and private interest groups at all levels.

ENABLING STEP

Meeting with appropriate organizations, the National Trust should determine how best to proceed in (a) implementing the collection, collation and analysis of existing standards pertaining to conservation in planning, design, program execution and subsequent management, operations and maintenance; and (b) organizing a national conference to establish an integrated system for preservation standards.

GOAL: CORRELATION

To achieve correlation between standards of preservation and applicable public law.

ENABLING STEPS
Heritage Conservation and Recreation Service (HCRS)
Collating existing federal regulations, codes and guidelines relating to preservation.

20

National Conference of State Historic Preservation Officers (NCSHPO)

Collating existing state and local regulations, codes and guidelines relating to preservation.

Convening statewide conferences, through the individual state historic preservation offices, to discuss with appropriate state and local code officials implementation of these changes.

HCRS and NCSHPO

Analyzing and evaluating the collated material to identify incompatibilities and working with appropriate officials to reconcile them.

Meeting jointly with the appropriate national organization of building officials to determine how best to incorporate changes at all levels.

GOAL: PRESERVATION AND PLANNING

To assure that preservation considerations are integrated into the continuing planning process of every community.

ENABLING STEP

Contacting appropriate governmental and nongovernmental organizations, such as the National League of Cities, National Conference of Mayors, National Association of Counties, International City Managers Association, American Planning Association, American Institute of Architects, American Society of Landscape Architects, American Society of Civil Engineers, the National Trust should seek to determine how best to (a) introduce preservation considerations into the planning process of every community; (b) prepare a cultural resources survey; (c) develop preservation plans; (d) provide adequate funding for professional staff and consultants to carry out the plans; and (e) include preservation considerations in management, maintenance and improvement programs.

GOAL: DIVERSE SKILLS

To develop guidelines governing sound practice that recognize preservation as an activity requiring many diverse skills.

ENABLING STEP

Consulting with the National Trust and the Heritage Conservation and Recreation Service, the Advisory Council on Historic Preservation should develop guidelines governing sound practices for professional, academic and vocational fields concerned with carrying out preservation projects.

GOAL: CULTURAL PROPERTY

To recognize that the concept of "cultural property" includes humanistic as well as physical qualities.

ENABLING STEP

Amending the National Historic Preservation Act of 1966 to expand the definition of "historic property" to include such humanistic concerns as folk, ethnic and traditional use patterns, to be initiated by the Advisory Council.

STANDARDS AND PRACTICES
Working Group

Helen Abell
William A. Baker
R. Michael Brown
Antoinette F. Downing
Charles H.P. Duell
Carl Feiss
Neal Fitzsimons*
Richard C. Frank, *Moderator**
B. Powell Harrison
Thomas J. Kane
James W. Lowell

Weiming Lu
Michael Middleton
W. Brown Morton III
Gordon D. Orr, Jr.
Judith Reynolds
Byron Rushing
Theodore A. Sande, *Recorder**
Arthur C. Townsend
Norman R. Weiss

Member, Editorial Review Committee

PRESERVATION: AVOCATION AND VOCATION

In the beginning, the American preservation movement was largely the domain of individuals whose preservation-related activities were avocational in nature. They formed the backbone of the preservation community. The success of these preservationists in awakening public interest in conservation of the built environment, in serving as stewards of significant properties and in lobbying for the passage of significant preservation legislation stimulated an increased demand for technical and managerial skills to meet increasingly complex problems. This situation has highlighted the interdependence of activist volunteers and career professionals. Preservation requires coordinated efforts of both the trained professional and the committed volunteer to resolve complex issues and to further the cause.

GOAL: MULTIDISCIPLINARY FIELD

To recognize that preservation is a multidisciplinary field requiring the skills and efforts of all concerned citizens and to capitalize on this rich diversity.

ENABLING STEP

Surveying types of preservation involvement, to be carried out by the National Trust.

MEANS OF IMPLEMENTATION

Identify existing and potential professional and nonprofessional involvements, specific talents and abilities that constitute the disciplines associated with preservation, to be carried out by the National Trust.

Identify capabilities of experienced preservation personnel who can be viewed as resource people in this process, to be carried out by the National Trust.

GOAL: DEFINITION OF ROLES, CRITERIA AND SKILLS

To study and define the roles, criteria and skills required for preservation activities by the career professional and the activist volunteer.

ENABLING STEP

Identifying the tasks that constitute the preservation field and the human resources involved in preservation activities at local, state and national levels.

MEANS OF IMPLEMENTATION

Identify those human resources through comprehensive and detailed surveys of preservation organizations, National Trust member organizations, federal and state review boards, local organizations and government bodies, planning agencies, professions and professional organizations.

Identify additional areas of needed expertise and their sources.

Develop lists of specialists in preservation and keep lists up to date.

ENABLING STEP

Coordinating efforts in the career professional and activist volunteer categories in order for preservation to reap maximum benefits from all participants.

MEANS OF IMPLEMENTATION

Establish performance standards and job descriptions and communicate them to all participants in preservation.

Use preservation conferences as a forum for exchange of information on tasks, roles and human resources.

Publish information on roles in national preservation organizations, e.g., on salaried positions, volunteer roles, etc.

GOAL: INCREASED VOLUNTEER PARTICIPATION

To increase activist volunteer participation in the preservation process.

ENABLING STEPS

Encouraging the role of the nonpaid participant.

Minimizing use of jargon by professionals that tends to intimidate the volunteer preservationist.

MEANS OF IMPLEMENTATION

Define the scope of the roles of paid and nonpaid preservationists.

Focus on involvement, contributions and interest of indig-

24

enous populations and current inhabitants of communities and neighborhoods.

Capitalize on docent or volunteer guide programs for tours, historical interpretation, etc.

Use qualified people to train inexperienced personnel.

Provide correct interpretive information for participants to disseminate to the public.

Evaluate training programs regularly.

ENABLING STEP

Developing and maintaining a recruitment program for non-paid participants to assure the continued growth and success of the preservation movement.

MEANS OF IMPLEMENTATION

Communicate preservation as a positive challenge and define its opportunities.

Encourage nonpaid participants to develop recruitment programs where needs are apparent.

Discuss volunteer activities in a *Preservation News* (monthly newspaper, National Trust) supplement, series of articles and/or National Trust *Information* sheet and in the commercial mass media.

ENABLING STEP

Developing an effective system of incentives and rewards to encourage participation of the nonpaid activist.

MEANS OF IMPLEMENTATION

Encourage preservation organizations to study individual incentive needs.

Create incentive programs (national, state, local) with awards, plaques, etc.

Prepare a manual on incentive programs, to be carried out by the National Trust.

GOAL: PROFESSIONAL MANAGEMENT

To develop a professional approach to the field of preservation management.

Identifying sources to help achieve quality management training.

Survey private management consulting firms for services available that would be helpful to preservation.

Survey graduate management programs that could offer studies useful in preservation management, e.g., accounting and personnel management.

Employ processes identified by the Standards and Practices working group.

ENABLING STEP

Encouraging appropriate compensation in relation to preservation job requirements.

MEANS OF IMPLEMENTATION

Survey and assess preservation organizations to identify job requirements and salary levels.

Disseminate information on job requirements and salary levels.

ENABLING STEP

Encouraging mid-career training and continuing education programs to focus on proper management for preservation organizations.

MEANS OF IMPLEMENTATION

Hold salaried administrators' conferences or continuing education seminars, to be carried out by the National Trust.

Communicate to nonprofit organizations the necessity for proper management for preservation organizations, to be carried out by the National Trust, American Association for State and Local History (AASLH) and National Park Service.

Develop more programs for historical agency and preservation agency management training, to be carried out by National Trust and AASLH.

Establish courses for preservation managers in university and continuing education programs through channels identified by the Education working group.

Communicate preservation management information through channels identified by the Communications working group.

PRESERVATION: AVOCATION AND VOCATION
Working Group

Helen Abell
Joan Williams Baldridge*
R. Michael Brown
Richard M. Candee
Antoinette F. Downing
James Marston Fitch
John B. Flowers III
Lynda C. Friedmann
Margot Gayle
Robert C. Giebner, *Moderator**
Roy E. Graham

Billie Harrington
Nancy H. Holmes
Christopher Owens
Anthony Reynolds
Joel B. Russ
Beatrice Utley*
Patricia E. Williams, *Recorder**

Member, Editorial Review Committee

27

EDUCATION

Preservation education needs to be based on a rational stewardship of diminishing cultural resources, an understanding of the relationship between the quality of the built environment and the quality of life and articulation of the value of a sense of time and place as a part of our diverse cultural memories. Further, preservation education must include local social, ethnic, economic, techological, environmental and cultural historical investigation in its curricula. It is necessary to improve preservation education, a process that will involve identifying existing educational models and, where missing, creating them; and working within existing educational systems and establishing better communication between teacher and student.

Public education for preservation should be based on activist volunteers and nonprofit community organizations continuing to play critical preservation roles assisted by preservation educators and universities and other cultural institutions making important public sector contributions to the preservation community. The significant contribution of volunteers to the historic preservation movement is fully recognized; their continued participation should be encouraged by responding to the demonstrated wish of the volunteer sector for greater professional assistance.

The early voluntary involvement of the educational sector in support of the preservation movement is almost unprecedented in the annals of American history. Thus far, in excess of $12 million has been invested by higher education institutions in support of the specialized needs of the field. The goals in education that follow respond to four major needs of the preservation movement: (1) to introduce preservation to students of the primary, secondary and collegiate levels; (2) to develop crafts training programs; (3) to support and strengthen advanced training in historic preservation to provide the professional expertise necessary to meet the needs of the field; and (4) to provide increased educational opportunities for the lay public and professional development programs for practicing professionals. To achieve the goals that will meet these needs will require financial resources beyond those now available to the educational sector. Therefore, utilization of existing agencies, organizations, programs and networks is encouraged, not only for reasons of economy, but for efficiency and practicality as well. At the same time, serious consideration should be given to the use of U.S. Department of the Interior preservation grants-in-aid on a matching basis.

The opportunity to implement these recommendations is dependent on a cooperative partnership among agencies such as the U.S. Department of the Interior in concert with other federal agencies: the U.S. Department of Education, the National Endowment for the Arts, the National Endowment for the Humanities and the National Folklife Center. Existing organizations that should assume a leadership role include the National Trust, the National Council for Preservation Education, the National Conference of State Historic Preservation Officers, the American Institute of Architects and the American Association for State and Local History.

GOAL: PRESERVATION ETHIC EDUCATION

To imbue succeeding generations of young Americans with the preservation ethic.

ENABLING STEPS

Introducing historic preservation concepts at primary and secondary school levels.

Training teachers to utilize historical resources in their teaching.

MEANS OF IMPLEMENTATION

Incorporate an understanding of America's built environment into existing teacher training programs.

Develop in-service training opportunities for teachers of environmental education, history, social studies, vocational education, art and other subjects where preservation can be made relevant.

ENABLING STEP

Introducing preservation concepts as a component of a general undergraduate education.

Encourage the development of one-semester courses in preservation in all U.S. colleges.

Strengthen the preservation component in traditional college disciplines such as history and art history.

Make introductory preservation courses interdisciplinary.

Create programs to foster a preservation awareness among faculty.

ENABLING STEP

Developing better classroom materials and assisting teachers in identifying community resources.

MEANS OF IMPLEMENTATION

Encourage publishers to develop textbooks that help students to understand the historical resources of their community and nation.

Interest state departments of education in adopting texts with this orientation.

Encourage local, state and regional preservation organizations and agencies to serve as resources and to help develop materials that will be of use to teachers and students.

GOAL: CRAFTS TRAINING PROGRAMS

To develop a variety of programs located throughout the country that would afford future artisans opportunities to acquire the necessary skills to conserve the nation's architectural heritage.

ENABLING STEP

Developing a partnership among vocational educators, museums, university preservation programs and preservation agencies and organizations.

MEANS OF IMPLEMENTATION

Provide assistance for vocational training for building craftspeople under supervision of experienced preservation practitioners.

Support master traditional craftspeople who can provide apprenticeship opportunities for vocational students.

Develop and disseminate appropriate building conservation

literature for vocational education teachers and students.

ENABLING STEP

Developing partnerships among trade union training programs, university preservation programs, contractors, building conservators, preservation agencies and organizations.

MEANS OF IMPLEMENTATION

Establish model programs within building trades apprenticeship programs to provide hands-on experience in quality rehabilitation.

Demonstrate to contractors the need to employ experienced, trained rehabilitation craftspeople.

Provide continuing education opportunities to develop craft skills and improve knowledge of building conservation practices.

GOAL: PROFESSIONAL EXPERTISE

To provide the professional expertise required for the conservation of the nation's cultural resources.

ENABLING STEP

Supporting and strengthening advanced professional training at the undergraduate and graduate levels in American colleges and universities.

MEANS OF IMPLEMENTATION

Promote the continued development of high quality advanced interdisciplinary training in such areas as building conservation, preservation planning, cultural resource management, historical and archeological research and the use of community resources in the classroom.

Develop and disseminate model preservation curricula, materials and resources through journals, conferences, clearinghouses, bibliographies and utilization of consortia.

Encourage support by the administrative sector in education to identify and make available the resources necessary to facilitate program improvement through such means as faculty development.

Recognize the significant contribution that practicing professionals can make to professional training programs through improvement of adjunct staff opportunities.

Promote increased cooperation between higher education and other preservation agencies and organizations through such means as intern programs and research contracts.

Provide continuing educational opportunities for professionals in preservation and allied fields.

GOAL: CONTINUING EDUCATION

To educate citizens involved in preservation, professionals in allied fields and public officials whose work affects historic resources on new developments in the preservation field.

ENABLING STEP

Developing continuing education opportunities for all interested citizens, including: property owners, leaders of local preservation organizations, heads of neighborhood groups, bankers, developers, investors, real estate agents, planning commission members, brokers, attorneys and chamber of commerce members.

MEANS OF IMPLEMENTATION

Make university programs available to fill the needs of the preservation community.

Develop, as needed, new short courses, workshops, institutes and conferences.

Encourage national and state professional organizations to cooperate with preservationists in training their members.

GOAL: FUNDING

To provide adequate seed money and funding to support the introduction of the preservation ethic into the nation's educational system.

ENABLING STEPS

Developing a direct matching fund program from federal agencies such as the U.S. Departments of the Interior and Education to the nation's educational institutions for development of a long-range preservation ethic.

Encouraging organizations that receive public funds to re-grant funds for education.

Encouraging preservation agencies and organizations to utilize the existing education programs.

EDUCATION
Working Group

Richard M. Candee*

Stephanie Churchill

Carol Clark

Richard K. Dozier

James Marston Fitch

John B. Flowers III

Nancy H. Holmes

James K. Huhta*

Roy F. Knight

Chester M. Liebs, *Moderator**

Elisabeth MacDougall

John Pearce

Roger L. Schluntz

Samuel N. Stokes, *Recorder**

Norman R. Weiss

William D. Wilkinson

Anthony C. Wood

Christopher Yip

**Member, Editorial Review Committee*

COMMUNICATIONS

The overall goal of communications is to deliver the preservation message in a clear, concise and forthright manner that will attract and hold the interest of the various constituencies that the preservation movement seeks to enlist. To do so the private preservation sector must increase public awareness and appreciation of preservation through communication within the movement and with the media. Media communication should emphasize preservation in all of its aspects, e.g., architecture, landscape architecture, archeology, maritime, etc. It also should seek to make preservation an integral part of land-use and urban planning and to integrate preservation into local and state planning processes.

Information programs in the private sector should be broadened to communicate more forcefully through publications and other media that preservation is part of the quality-of-life movement. Links to other quality-of-life organizations such as the Sierra Club, Nature Conservancy and Trust for Public Land should be strengthened. Preservation must be made a part of the political process so that candidates will speak on preservation issues and organizations will publicize and, when possible, lobby for them.

GOAL: PRIMARY MESSAGE

To clarify and broaden the preservation movement's primary message, to improve the quality of life in America and to identify the movement more clearly as part of that overall effort.

ENABLING STEP

Establishing a communications network in the preservation movement in which local, state and regional preservation organizations identify one individual to serve as public information officer; these officers then serve as a formal communications network for the movement.

MEANS OF IMPLEMENTATION

Forward information on important local, state or regional developments to the National Trust Office of Public Affairs to spot emerging trends or issues within the movement. The National Trust would use this information to inform national news outlets on the issues, resulting in benefits to preservation that would include widespread discussion of the issues and national publicity for local preservation organizations.

Encourage editors and reporters of more than 1,000 existing preservation publications to focus on the need to communicate the primary preservation message, i.e., that preservation is part of the quality-of-life movement.

Urge editors and reporters within the preservation movement to communicate the quality-of-life message as part of their efforts.

Identify environmental organizations and government bodies that embrace the quality-of-life message and strengthen contacts with their public affairs staffs by exchanging publications, jointly attending and participating in annual meetings and by forming coalitions for accomplishing similar quality-of-life goals of the built and natural environments.

Use *Preservation News* (monthly newspaper, National Trust) to inform preservation organizations that improving the quality of life is the single most important communications goal.

GOAL: COMMUNICATIONS CHANNELS

To use all communications channels, especially the commercial mass media, at greatly increased levels.

ENABLING STEP

Conducting a general market survey to determine the public's attitude toward preservation in order to maximize the effectiveness of media efforts.

MEANS OF IMPLEMENTATION

Expand national television coverage, including news and special features.

Increase national print media coverage, including general interest as well as business and financial magazines.

GOAL: PRESERVATION AND THE POLITICAL PROCESS

To insert a preservation point of view into the political process through communications and public relations techniques.

ENABLING STEPS

Ascertaining political candidates' views on preservation.

Providing preservation information to candidates who are likely to support preservation.

Encouraging preservationists to run for public office.

Recommending that elected officials appoint preservationists to government positions.

MEANS OF IMPLEMENTATION

Have lobbying organizations publicly rate elected officials on their preservation positions.

Plan more aggressive lobbying programs.

Attract the interest of politicians with more effective use of the economic rationale for preservation activity.

GOAL: AUDIENCES

To identify particular audiences, shaping the preservation message to suit their particular interests and communicating it aggressively.

ENABLING STEPS

Reshaping the communications approach of preservation to make it factual and supported by statistical data.

Gathering necessary statistical data to support preservation's claims for energy conservation and urban and neighborhood rehabilitation.

Surveying for their interests and concerns: business and financial groups, corporate executives, service clubs, chambers of commerce, state historic preservation officers, banks, insurance companies, mortgage bankers, real estate developers and the tourist industry.

Forming alliances with like-minded groups in all socioeconomic segments of society in order to strengthen the preservation movement's foundation.

36

Communicating aggressively to advocacy organizations such as those representing minorities, ethnic groups, community activists and neighborhood residents.

MEANS OF IMPLEMENTATION

Use communications tools such as organizations' internal publications, trade publications, annual meetings and films.

Urge the National Trust to develop models for shaping preservation messages for particular audiences.

GOAL: TERMINOLOGY COMMUNICATION

To communicate to the preservation community and the general public the meaning of preservation terms with which there is a lack of familiarity.

ENABLING STEP

Preparing short, specific and positive messages on the meaning of the terms.

MEANS OF IMPLEMENTATION

Communicate the terms' concepts through the commercial mass media and public relations officers of environmental-preservation organizations, corporations and government agencies.

GOAL: PRESERVATION ACTIVITIES

To intensify the exposure of the variety of activities within the preservation movement.

ENABLING STEP

Developing information on the variety of activities and people in the preservation movement.

MEANS OF IMPLEMENTATION

Use the commercial mass media and public relations officers of environmental-preservation organizations, corporations and government agencies to report on these activities and people.

GOAL: PRESERVATION EDUCATION AWARENESS

To promote public awareness of, sensitivity toward and appreciation for preservation education.

ENABLING STEP

Influencing the public through cultural institutions, television, radio, newspapers, newsletters, brochures, journals, magazines, seminars and community service projects.

GOAL: FUNDING AND SUPPORT

To have local, state and national preservation groups earmark adequate financial and human resources to accomplish communications goals in a professional manner.

ENABLING STEPS

Developing shared communications responsibility among preservation groups on national, state and local levels.

Developing good pilot projects and case studies to prove preservation's merits and undertaking studies in economic benefits, energy savings and efficiency, social effects, neighborhood revitalization, etc. (Where studies already exist, such as those of the National Endowment for the Arts and the National Trust, they should be made known to local preservation groups.)

GOAL: COMMUNICATIONS SKILLS

To raise the professional level of preservation communicators.

ENABLING STEPS

Developing seminars for the private preservation sector on effective communications techniques and skills.

Using internal publications to enhance communications in the private preservation sector.

Using professional public relations, marketing and advertising consultants more effectively to sell the private preservation movement, as the creative and imaginative sellers of soap and toothpaste do.

COMMUNICATIONS
Working Group

Robert Berkebile

James Biddle

Charles M. Black, *Moderator**

Porter Briggs

Calvin Carter

William A.V. Cecil

Bruce Chapman

Franklin P. Conaway

Dana Crawford

Beverly Fluty

Roderick S. French

Roy F. Knight

Robert A. Puckett

Beverly Reece

Joseph A. Satrom*

James R. Short

Lyn Snoddon, *Recorder**

Frank H. Spink, Jr.

Margot Wellington

William H. Whyte, Jr.

J. Reid Williamson

Member, Editorial Review Committee

39

INFORMATION RESOURCES

As a movement historic preservation and the areas of its involvement are constantly changing. It lacks a generally accepted philosophy, as well as goals and scope. Thus, it is difficult to develop an information management system because of the diversity of subject areas involved and the need for the latest information.

All too frequently the quality of basic preservation information materials is substandard; often the content is incompletely developed and has a narrow focus. The result is information that tends to lead to characterizations of the preservationist as a "fuzzy-headed obstructionist." The defects that result in such material include the following: propaganda and boosterism without critical evaluation of goals, methods and results; lack of accurate research and in-depth information; value judgments that bias reporting; and lack of a systematic procedure to identify information gaps in key preservation areas.

The huge volume of preservation information supposedly available is not easily accessible to most preservationists because it is not assembled, organized and synthesized for use in a timely and meaningful manner. The development of appropriate information resources and a system for their management is predicated on the development of a generally accepted preservation philosophy. As the philosophy develops, a system can be created to assure broad-based access to information and to offset the high costs and inefficiency of many uncoordinated, independent information sources.

GOAL: INFORMATION SYSTEMS NETWORK

To develop a network of information management systems that are not necessarily centralized but that are compatible on the local, state, regional and national levels.

ENABLING STEPS

Identifying and defining terminology and developing descriptors by which to index information.

Creating, maintaining and updating: (a) an indexing system

that identifies published and unpublished materials, resource people and groups, artifacts; (b) an analysis system that identifies existing and future users and their needs; and (c) an organization system with standardized indexes to permit accessibility and efficient cross-indexing and multi-indexing.

Establishing retrieval and dissemination systems that, where possible, utilize existing information centers.

INFORMATION RESOURCES
Working Group

Stephanie Churchill
Susan Dewitt
Donald Dworsky
Beverly Fluty
Charles B. Hosmer, Jr.
Jeffrey Jahns
Carleton Knight III, *Recorder**
Wayne A. Linker
William J. Murtagh
Beverly Reece

Anthony Reynolds
Byron Rushing
Joel B. Russ
Ann Webster Smith
Miriam Trementozzi, *Moderator**
Conrad True
Russell Wright

Member, Editorial Review Committee

TERMINOLOGY

There is a need to continue redefining preservation terms and concepts because they have myriad connotations for many different groups; even the terms "historic preservation" and "preservation" are troublesome. Historic preservation as a movement risks dilution if it is made to be everything to everyone. Today, the movement has advanced into the area of neighborhood revitalization by affecting large numbers of historic buildings in a single area. Thus, the preservation movement needs to define its role and functions in neighborhoods. Is its concern merely the physical fabric or will it influence social patterns? Preservation, on the other hand, has a wider emphasis that goes beyond historic buildings; it includes all aspects of the cultural, social and physical environments. In some cases a special ambience or ethnic quality may be the dominant value of an area, superseding that of architectural presence. A process to study, review and manage terminology is needed.

GOAL: UNDERSTANDING TERMINOLOGY

To develop a clear understanding of the various connotations of preservation terminology held by the public, technicians and professionals and to establish definitions.

ENABLING STEPS

Establishing a broadly based, geographically distributed group to: look at sample materials, identify terms and collect a sampling of data on usage; develop a list of preservation-related terms, research current connotations by identifying users and programs that influence preservation-related terms and written sources; and assemble findings and connotations.

Completing a glossary of preservation terms, a publication planned by the National Trust.

Culling preservation process words from the papers presented at both the Chicago 1978 annual meeting Future Directions Symposia and the Williamsburg conference.

GOAL: TERMINOLOGY SYSTEM

To develop a system to disseminate, test and modify terminology.

ENABLING STEPS

Selecting from previously compiled lists individuals and organizations who use preservation-related words to help develop a system.

Publishing and distributing the preliminary terminology to the preservation constituency and related disciplines for review and comments.

Documenting and coordinating reactions to the terminology.

Modifying terminology as needed.

GOAL: PUBLISH TERMINOLOGY

To publish the final terminology and promote its usage within the preservation constituency and related disciplines.

ENABLING STEP

Distributing the terminology to communicators within the preservation movement and other communications professionals (i.e., advertising, public relations, public affairs, corporate communicators) and monitoring and commenting on terminology usage by the public media.

MEANS OF IMPLEMENTATION

Have the National Trust assume a leadership role in the applied use of terminology.

GOAL: ONGOING REVIEW AND REVISION

To establish mechanisms that will assure an ongoing preservation-related terminology review and revision process.

ENABLING STEPS

Utilizing the initial group of compilers to: review terminology and eliminate noncontested terms; identify and research variations of contested terms; establish revised definitions; and disseminate revisions.

TERMINOLOGY
Working Group

Stephanie Churchill
Susan Dewitt
Donald Dworsky
Beverly Fluty
Charles B. Hosmer, Jr.
Jeffrey Jahns
Carleton Knight III, *Recorder**
Wayne A. Linker
William J. Murtagh
Beverly Reece

Anthony Reynolds
Byron Rushing
Joel B. Russ
Ann Webster Smith
Miriam Trementozzi, *Moderator**
Conrad True
Russell Wright

**Member, Editorial Review Committee*

FUNDING

Preservation requires funding from both public and private sources, and every available policy option and business approach should be exploited. Development of new institutions to provide preservation financing should be encouraged as they are needed, but priority should be given to making the existing infrastructure work more effectively. While the quantity of funds available is important, the reliability (i.e., the consistency and continuity) of these funds is critical.

Public policy at all levels should have a fundamental predisposition toward preservation because public policy often determines how private funds are committed. The consideration of and funding for preservation projects should be integrated into the policies of each agency at all levels of government.

GOAL: RELIABLE LONG-TERM BASIS

To establish funding on a reliable long-term basis from a variety of private and public sources for the full range of preservation activities.

ENABLING STEP

Identifying in a single reference work the sources of and techniques for funding the broad range of preservation programs.

MEANS OF IMPLEMENTATION

Develop and maintain through the National Trust a current reference that identifies sources of funds, describes how to apply for them and how the funds might be used in preservation projects and provides case histories of innovative projects.

ENABLING STEP

Measuring the economic, social and cultural costs and benefits of preservation activities to date and measuring the magnitude of preservation work to be done.

45

MEANS OF IMPLEMENTATION

Assemble and analyze economic and other relevant data, with the National Trust as coordinator, to provide studies for justifying funding programs. Sources of data on costs and benefits include unions, planners, civic and trade associations, developers and historic district commissions as well as preservation groups.

ENABLING STEP

Encouraging greater financial support for the administration of nonprofit preservation programs.

MEANS OF IMPLEMENTATION

Conduct, through the National Trust, coordinated, joint fund-raising programs with local preservation organizations, including solicitation of corporations and foundations. Mechanisms should be developed to document the local value of corporate gifts to nonprofit preservation organizations.

Make direct grants or loans from the National Trust and the Heritage Conservation and Recreation Service to local organizations for the sole purpose of fund raising.

Encourage the expansion of the National Endowment for the Arts and the National Endowment for the Humanities challenge grant programs.

ENABLING STEP

Encouraging the formation of equity capital pools to initiate preservation projects.

MEANS OF IMPLEMENTATION

Utilize philanthropic funds for "front-end" costs to determine preservation feasibility.

Utilize portions of the National Trust endowment for equity financing for preservation projects.

Develop and introduce legislation to allow nonprofit preservation organizations to issue tax-exempt bonds to provide equity capital for preservation projects.

ENABLING STEP

Developing greater awareness of and expertise in preservation within the federal government leading to flexible programs to supplement funds from the private sector.

46

MEANS OF IMPLEMENTATION

Establish a mechanism for regular communication among federal agency representatives involved in preservation.

Educate congressional and executive branch leaders on the existence of the preservation constituency.

GOAL: EQUAL ECONOMIC CHOICE

To establish at least equal economic choices between utilizing older structures and replacing them.

ENABLING STEP

Developing strategies to make preservation more competitive with other development activities.

MEANS OF IMPLEMENTATION

Examine and expand current preservation incentives and demolition disincentives contained in legislation at all levels of government.

Examine the effectiveness of the preservation provisions of the Tax Reform Act of 1976 and the Revenue Act of 1978.

Develop preservation tax incentives for residential properties through legislation for the benefit of both owners and · tenants.

Strengthen penalties at all levels of government for the unnecessary demolition of historic properties.

Study the utilization of demolition permit fees to discourage demolition and encourage creation of a funding source to support preservation.

ENABLING STEP

Stressing the relationship of preservation to broad national policy concerns such as employment, energy conservation and reuse of existing infrastructures.

MEANS OF IMPLEMENTATION

Encourage further studies to examine relative labor intensiveness and energy efficiency of, and demand on, existing utilities by preservation as opposed to new construction.

ENABLING STEP

Developing additional nongovernmental strategies to fund preservation projects.

Encourage syndicated projects to develop equity capital.

Utilize nonprofit corporations to develop project analysis, making the case for preservation and rehabilitation and reducing "front-end" exposure for developers.

Develop stronger lobbying efforts with state and local civic organizations to demand greater financial support for preservation work.

Encourage a better understanding of grantsmanship to promote new financial support for preservation work.

Reinforce small community businesses as both owners and tenants of historic buildings.

ENABLING STEP

Expanding the role of the National Trust in making preservation more competitive with other economic forces.

MEANS OF IMPLEMENTATION

Establish an economic advisory board staffed with persons knowledgeable in real estate finance and development, to evaluate local project proposals and advise on their economic viability.

Examine National Trust policies of continued ownership and administration of house museums.

Study the concept of a National Bank for Historic Preservation.

Expand the National Trust Endangered Properties Program.

Explore National Trust participation as a direct financial partner in preservation projects.

GOAL: PUBLIC PRESERVATION POLICY

To base public policy at all levels on a fundamental predisposition toward preservation.

ENABLING STEP

Developing social accounting policies that consider preservation benefits and that are uniformly applied throughout the country.

MEANS OF IMPLEMENTATION

Develop in federal agencies involved in preservation, with input from state and local public and private preservation groups, a standard for evaluating in-place structures and the costs to preserve them against the cost and suitability of replacing them.

Utilize federal legislative and fiscal leverage to create a predisposition to preservation at the state and local government levels.

ENABLING STEP

Creating executive and legislative mechanisms at all levels of government to implement standards to evaluate in-place structures vis-a-vis replacement structures.

MEANS OF IMPLEMENTATION

Urge state and local governments to pursue preservation policies by linking the availability of federal funds to performance measured against established standards.

Develop stronger state and local legislation establishing preservation as a public policy.

FUNDING
Working Group

Betts Abel
Leopold Adler II
James Biddle
Dana Crawford
Kathy Dexter
V. Rodger Digilio*
Donald Dworsky
Carl Feiss
Richard C.D. Fleming
Richard W. Freeman, Jr., *Moderator*
Lynda C. Friedmann
John L. Frisbee, *Recorder*
Mel Gamzon
Stephen S. Halsey
John E. Hansel

Billie Harrington
B. Powell Harrison
Annabelle Heath
J. Myrick Howard
Jeffrey Jahns
James W. Lowell
Kenneth Orenstein
Jeffrey J. Park
Jan Thorman
Conrad True
Roger W. Webb
J. Reid Williamson
Arthur P. Ziegler, Jr.

*Member,
Editorial Review Committee*

LEGISLATION

A preservation agenda for the 1980s should place more emphasis on efforts at the state and local levels to balance a tendency during the last decade to look at preservation from the federal viewpoint. To this end a meaningful legislative agenda must place a stronger emphasis on citizen participation, citizen initiation, citizen access to the system and, above all, citizen responsibility. Much legislation favorable to preservation has been passed at all levels of government in recent years. It cannot be assumed, however, that each level of government will do as well in the future; there are still weak links in the preservation chain. It is apparent that state efforts and capabilities could be strengthened, and that state and local efforts should be more closely related and mutually supportive.

Initiatives to encourage the use of legislation at the local level should be strengthened. Many cities and counties have not yet utilized their present preservation capability, perhaps because local governments have not always understood the importance of preservation as a source of strength in the local economy or the significance of preservation as a cause of political importance to local citizens. This is essentially an educational and political problem that precedes the effective use of legislative tools. However, where the problem is one of inadequate state enabling legislation for use by cities and counties, strong efforts must be made at the state level to provide effective legislation. In both cases, experience with federal programs during the last decade should be useful and instructive in approaching the development of stronger preservation programs at the local level.

The last 10 years have been marked by the rapid growth of private preservation organizations, both local and state. It is important that the legislative initiatives for preservation in the 1980s support and enhance the ability of these organizations to play their increasingly important roles in historic preservation.

GOAL: PRESERVATION ORGANIZATION INITIATIVE

To encourage initiatives by private preservation organizations at the state and local levels and to strengthen their overall capability.

ENABLING STEPS
Private Preservation Organizations

Taking a more aggressive role in influencing public action, through example and through the media, by participating more actively in local and state planning processes, by educating the public and by demonstrating the feasibility of preservation through innovative techniques.

Seeking or supporting legislative initiatives that strengthen organizations' capability to act, especially through such private law techniques as preservation restrictions and easements.

Seeking and being given an increased share of public funding to carry out their programs.

Taking an active role in monitoring federal and state programs, supporting those programs that have proven themselves and recommending change or improvements in those programs when change or improvement is needed.

Lending support to legislative initiatives that strengthen public preservation programs at every level of government.

Working to support increased public funding for preservation projects.

GOAL: PRESERVATION/RELATED GROUPS' EFFECTIVENESS

To increase the effectiveness of state and local private preservation organizations in working with other related groups and interests.

ENABLING STEPS

Taking necessary steps to clarify private preservation organizations' right of access to the judicial system; it is important that the standing to sue of private organizations be clear in each state.

Recognizing and encouraging the preservation of neighborhood identity when making legislative initiatives.

Respecting both the rights of residents and the processes of democratic self-government in legislative efforts involving preservation organizations in neighborhood preservation programs.

Seeking through legislative initiatives to expand the capacity of private organizations to provide technical assistance to neighborhood preservation constituencies and supporting the ability of neighborhood groups to act on their own.

Recognizing in working with neighborhood groups that preservation of historical and architectural values may be only one of many important issues in the community.

Having private preservation organizations be accessible and encouraging clear identification and open discussion of local preservation issues in governmental and private forums.

GOAL: CAPABILITY OF LOCAL GOVERNMENTS

To strengthen the capacity of local governments to carry out more effective historic preservation programs.

ENABLING STEPS
Private Sector

Seeking increased federal, state and local government support for local public preservation efforts that are often the weak link in the preservation chain.

Utilizing systems now in existence for review of alterations and new construction in historic districts, systems that are generally adequate in substance and procedure.

Undertaking legislative initiatives at the state and local levels, as necessary, to bring up to the highest standards the preservation review process as it relates to surveys, evaluations, nominations and designations in each state.

Assuring that new initiatives for public preservation programs in the areas of regulation and financial support are politically realistic and legally defensible.

Focusing evolution of local regulatory systems, which often create an adversary relationship between the public and private sectors, on mediation and arbitration models, emphasizing opportunities for negotiation.

52

GOAL: DEVOLUTION OF RESPONSIBILITY

To seek a devolution of responsibility for administering public historic preservation programs from the federal government to states and localities.

ENABLING STEPS
State and Local Governments

Providing greater authority and responsibility for the identification and nomination of cultural resources to the National Register of Historic Places.

Allowing greater flexibility in the use of grant-in-aid funds.

Promoting more active involvement in the federal planning and decision-making processes affecting historic properties.

Encouraging greater recognition of preservation concerns in land-use planning and management processes.

Establishing the necessary capability to accept increased responsibility for public preservation programs; in many communities the public-private preservation partnership must be strengthened.

Strengthening efforts to obtain legislation supportive of a balanced public-private preservation effort will be necessary in those states where the legislative base for preservation is weak.

Recognizing that any devolution of federal activities places a corresponding responsibility on states and localities to assure that the purposes of federal preservation legislation will be respected.

MEANS OF IMPLEMENTATION

Begin a broad-based effort to sensitize, educate and motivate state and local preservation constituencies to the need for given legislative initiatives, involving elected and appointed public officials and the business and political communities as well as preservationists. In some states, this will require more effective lobbying efforts than now exist, and it should rely to a greater extent on nontraditional sources of support such as unions and ethnic groups.

Prepare and disseminate materials that convincingly demonstrate the benefits of preservation to state and local legislators; this is a special responsibility of private national organizations such as the National Trust. Wherever possible, the National Trust should play a supporting role when state and local legislative initiatives are at stake.

Provide, through the states and the National Trust, more forums for the discussion of experience with state and local preservation legislation.

Expand technical assistance to local preservation comissions.

Encourage the development of greater expertise by practicing attorneys in the field of preservation law, especially at the local level.

Develop and disseminate widely information and guidance on state and local preservation legislation and legal techniques.

Obtain cooperation from national private organizations and government agencies in carrying out these efforts.

LEGISLATION
Working Group

Minnette C. Bickel	Douglas A. Johnston
Tersh Boasberg	Lawson B. Knott, Jr.
Peter H. Brink	Nellie L. Longsworth
Paul S. Byard	William K. Reilly
Bruce Chapman	Jerry L. Rogers
John J. Costonis	Robert E. Stipe, *Moderator**
Carl Feiss	Diana Waite
John M. Fowler*	Frederick C. Williamson
Roderick S. French	Anne St. Clair Wright
Frank B. Gilbert, *Recorder**	
Mardi Gualtieri	*Member, Editorial Review Committee*

PART 2:
SPECIAL PRESENTATIONS

THE ECONOMIC AND SOCIAL RETURNS OF PRESERVATION

John Kenneth Galbraith

The preservation movement has one great curiosity. There is never any retrospective controversy or regret. Preservationists are the only people in the world who are invariably confirmed in their wisdom after the fact. This is illustrated by a remembrance from my childhood. When growing up in Canada, I shared with my compatriots a disdain for the only architectural form Canadians ever developed, namely, that great manifestation known as Canadian Pacific Railway Gothic, of which a superlative example is the Toronto City Hall. Then, a few years ago, I found myself on the committee to save for posterity the building I had always been required as a reputable student in Ontario to regard with lofty contempt. Today, nothing gives me more pleasure than to go back to Toronto and hear everybody applauding the fact that the building is now safe forever.

In almost all cases there is also approval of this type of effort on narrow economic grounds. The reason for economic approval is, of course, that nothing so attracts people in our time as the architectural wonders of the past. Natural wonders are a poor second and, in some degree, peculiar to the United States or the Western Hemisphere. Being a relatively new society, we have tended, in the absence of a great wealth of architectural treasures, to concentrate on such natural wonders as the Grand Canyon, Yosemite and Yellowstone national parks and, in past times, Niagara Falls. People reward the communities near these sights with their money in the process of seeing them.

The great attraction of all travel is to see things that deliberately, by accident or by the continuity of institutions, as in the case of the church, have been saved for the present generation. The fact that Americans by the tens and hundreds of thousands travel overseas each year should not surprise anyone, and no one should be surprised at what they seek

John Kenneth Galbraith is professor emeritus of economics at Harvard University, Cambridge, Mass.

out. They do not seek out the natural beauty of the British countryside, attractive as that is. They seek things that have been conserved deliberately in continuity with the past. And they look, also, at the monuments of past despotism.

The Economic Reward in India

India, where I served as ambassador not long ago, provides an example of how the aftermath of conservation pays a large economic reward. Two things have changed India from an economic burden to one of the strong economies of our time. One is the export of the educated unemployed to the rest of the world and the return of the revenues therefrom; the other is the large flow of people who come to India to see the antiquities and the architectural masterpieces.

This is a splendid tribute to the conservation movement. The man who was responsible for it was George Curzon, viceroy of India at the turn of the century. During his rule Curzon sensed that a great wealth of art and architecture was being lost. The Taj Mahal was being looted of its semi-precious stones and marble; the great caves at Ajanta and Ellora were similarly suffering, with the marvelous Ajanta cave paintings being recklessly exposed and photographed and ruined in the process.

It was Curzon who established the Indian Department of Archeology, which ever since has done a remarkable job of historic preservation. In consequence of that activity, there has been a flow of travelers to India to see these wonders that has paid over and over again the costs of their initial protection and subsequent care. But the economics of conservation and preservation encompasses two problems we must never forget.

While the return in the narrow economic sense will almost always be greater than the initial cost, the time dimension runs unfavorably to this effort, as illustrated by Curzon's conservation activity. It was 50 to 75 years before the economic return began to reach a full flood in India. No one should expect such return—and most particularly that from visitors, travellers and tourism—to be immediate. It will, and perhaps even should, develop over time.

The other infinitely serious and difficult problem concerning the economics of preservation is the disjunction of

58

interests that are involved. The people who ultimately reap the economic reward are not the people—or only by accident are they the people—who have the immediate interest in the object in question. This is something that again is illustrated by the Taj Mahal. There was considerable interest in removing the semiprecious stones and the marble that had so marvelously created that structure and selling them to the first tourist to come along.

Saving a Castle

One of the great acts of preservation was that of a castle built by the Knights of St. John of the Hospital about 100 miles north of Damascus on a mountain peak commanding a pass near the Mediterranean Sea. It is a structure of unbelievable magnificence, a great keep, an inner castle with a curtain wall around. During their mandate under the League of Nations, the French wanted to assure that it would be kept. But there was conflict because the castle was a great source of cut stone for the surrounding community.

Again, the immediate loss was to the people for whom the castle represented a nearly inexhaustible supply of raw material, and the ultimate gain was for the people who now come to see this most wonderful of castles.

New York and Newport

A simpler case over which preservationists should weep is New York City's Fifth Avenue. One of the tragedies of the preservation movement in the United States is that the great houses on Fifth Avenue have been lost. There was a disjunction of interests there between the people who owned the real estate, those who could make money from building apartment houses and those who wanted to make Fifth Avenue what it was at the beginning of this century—one of the too few architectural wonders of the Western world. The cost to private owners of maintaining the great houses on Fifth Avenue was simply too high and the opportunity for revenue from other buildings was too tempting. The houses were torn down over the decades and replaced by far from distinguished apartment buildings.

Newport, R.I., reflects a slightly different problem. Changing styles and changing family fortunes made the wonderful houses there an expense few families could continue to sustain. But fortunately the area did not have an alternative real estate value. And by the time people became aware of the wonders of Newport, the preservation movement had reached the point where a large number of the houses were saved.

The Market and Preservation

Preservationists must never be beguiled by the notion that we can rely on natural economic forces or that we can rely on the market. If they do, a large number of important art objects, artifacts and buildings will be sacrificed. The reason is that the market works on a short-time dimension and the people who respond to the market are different from those who ultimately gain from conservation or preservation.

The market works against social economic interest as well as the larger interest in the artistic and educational rewards of conservation. This is not a question of ideology and should not be thought of as an argument between liberals and conservatives. It is a simple fact that the market will always favor the short-run solution—the people pulling the stones out of the Taj Mahal. It will always favor the people who are in immediate possession, as against the large social and economic interests of the community. Preservationists must never doubt that they are engaged in a public and philanthropic and social enterprise and should never, whatever their political faith, be in the slightest degree apologetic.

Any time it is suggested that these are matters that can be left to the free play of private enterprise, it is the obligation of everybody associated with this movement, whatever the person's political faith, to rise up in indignation and say, "You don't know what you're talking about." This is not a question of ideology; it is a question of hard circumstance.

The Veblen Story

There also should be no doubt that there are cultural, educational and aesthetic values that are well beyond the range of economic calculation and that assure us we are right. This leads to one last example and that concerns the case of the Veblen homestead. Thorstein Veblen was born in Wisconsin, but was raised in southern Minnesota in a

60

beautiful farmhouse that was built by Thomas Veblen, his father. Thorstein Veblen's *The Theory of the Lesiure Class* and his subsequent books, *The Theory of Business Enterprise* and *Higher Learning in America,* changed not only the way people thought but the way they lived.

The Theory of the Leisure Class is a mordant, ironic examination of the social mores of the great American rich. From that book come the phrases "conspicuous consumption," "conspicuous leisure" and "pecuniary emulation." The consequence of Veblen's work, the need to avoid conspicuous consumption and conspicuous leisure, had a devastating effect on the rich. They had to spend less in order to avoid what Veblen said was bad taste but which was also something perilously similar to what, orgiastically, an anthropologist might find a Papuan chief doing. And they had also to find employment because leisure became unworthy.

A few years ago we filmed a segment of the television series "The Age of Uncertainty" at the Veblen farm. I was distressed to see this structure in the last stage of disrepair. And I was distressed for another reason. The farm is living evidence of one of the errors in the interpretation of Veblen. It was long held that his reaction was that of the poor boy against the rich; that he was motivated by class envy. One had to see the marvelous richness of that farm to know that that was not true. The Veblens were not poor; they were thrifty and hardworking. By the standards of anything that Thomas Veblen, who came from Norway, had ever known, they were people of modest affluence.

When we finished filming, I returned to nearby Northfield, Minn. One day I went to the local museum and discovered that they had never heard of Thorstein Veblen. The person they celebrated with a substantial exhibit was the other great figure of the town—Jesse James.

It was out of a feeling that Jesse James should share some of the esteem in a civilized community with the greatest sociologist of our country that I was led to join with others in an effort to do something to preserve the Veblen homestead.

I wrote a letter to Wendell Anderson, then governor of Minnesota, telling something of the role of Veblen in Minnesota history. I described to him at length the marvelous

way in which the house where Adam Smith lived is preserved in Edinburgh, as are the houses where Hume and
others lived. I asked why Scandinavians were so negligent
of their great.

Anderson got in touch with the Minnesota Historical
Society and urged it to do something about the homestead.
The result was a large meeting in Minnesota; several hundred
people turned up for a lecture on Thorstein Veblen. Out of
this effort at historic site preservation* came not an economic return but an important lesson in political tactics.
Even ethnic pride can be exploited.

Nothing has given me more pleasure than to have these
efforts rewarded by the knowledge that this lovely old house
in its beautiful countryside will be there from now on.

* The Veblen home has been preserved with the help of a National Trust loan and
a grant from the Minnesota State Historic Preservation Office enabling a local
organization to buy the original 1868 frame house, barn, granary and 10 acres of
land. National Trust help was provided through its Endangered Properties Program,
which responds to immediate threats to significant landmarks.

PRESERVING OUR NATIONAL IDENTITY: A FEDERAL AGENCY VIEW

Jane Yarn

Historic preservation is a subject of critical interest to the Council on Environmental Quality. The council is one of the few federal agencies blessed not only with a single statutory charter but with one that is gratifyingly concise— the National Environmental Policy Act of 1969 (NEPA). It is CEQ's responsibility to oversee federal agency efforts to achieve NEPA's goals and to meet the act's procedural requirements. One NEPA goal stands out as most pertinent. It is that federal agencies should "preserve important historic, cultural and natural aspects of our national heritage and maintain, wherever possible, an environment which supports diversity and variety of individual choice." This important, relevant and challenging goal is one that the federal government certainly has not achieved, but one that I believe should shape the agenda of the preservation movement in the 1980s.

Although I doubt that anyone would dispute the desirability of this particular goal for federal agencies, it is worth emphasizing some of its basic assumptions:

That our national heritage includes a mix of historic, cultural and natural resources that cannot be separated.

That these resources should be protected to produce an environment that is diverse—ecologically and socially.

That this diversity should be maintained both economically and ecologically over a long period of time.

That there is a need to maintain a variety of individual choices.

Choosing Social Ends

As a nation, we have not pursued this NEPA goal with sufficient energy or persistence. Too often our development patterns and our newly acquired ways of living suggest quite the contrary. Some years ago, Russell Baker illustrated this

Jane Yarn is a member of the Council on Environmental Quality, Washington, D.C.

disturbing phenomenon with an observation on the shopping center:

> There is only one shopping center in existence. . . . It moves around the continent at the speed of light. You find it at Wheaton, Md., and then—get on an airplane and fly like a bullet to escape the horror of it— there it is waiting for you at Irving, Tex., or Falmouth, Mass.
>
> Or, maybe it isn't moving around the country at all. Maybe it truly is everywhere. Maybe America really is a shopping center. . . . Asphalt, stolidly menacing shelves of homogeneity marching off to a cement horizon; hot dogs and self-service, mass-produced people and neon, a market with no smells. ("Vanishing America," *The New York Times*)

The shopping center symbolizes the complexity of our quest to preserve natural, cultural and historical values, diversity and broad choices. Shopping centers, as much as any other development, have had disastrous direct effects on historic landmarks and traditional ways of life. Just as important, they have indirectly weakened the economy of nearby towns or urban centers with historic and cultural attributes. They have been allowed to have these effects, of course, because they serve other desired social ends— ends that preservationists must recognize.

Grappling with Neglected Forces

If preservationists have any hope of addressing future problems posed by the social and physical changes of the 1980s, an essential step is to understand and grapple with economic, demographic and political forces heretofore often neglected.

We can start by being aware of the pressures on and responses of the federal government. Despite the important laws and Executive Orders designed since the mid-1960s to protect cultural and historic resources, federal agencies still contribute substantially to the loss of these resources, directly and indirectly. For example, decisions about the location of federal post offices still have significant impact on the economic vitality of old urban areas and small towns. Water projects still flood historic properties, as the New Melones Dam in northern California will do. Interstate highways and beltways are planned for urban areas that will, if the past is any guide, radically accelerate or change suburban growth patterns and alter historic landscapes around our cities in the process. New shopping centers will be stimulated by roads and water and sewer lines in rural areas

64

funded by several agencies, often quite intentionally, to spur rural "development."

Recent demographic trends in the United States appear to cause and stimulate the federal projects just mentioned. The startling reversal of migration patterns and the rapid growth of our most rural areas since 1970 reflect new second homes, recreational and retirement interests, easier transportation and availability of manufacturing, mining, educational and other jobs. The new rural settlers appear not to choose old dwelling sites and town living, but to prefer dispersal that resembles a kind of "buckshot" pattern. As a result, our small towns, our scenic forests and our agricultural landscapes are undergoing significant change, often to the detriment of historic rural values.

How will the federal government respond to these trends? In the past, federal efforts have been directed toward spurring rural growth in traditional ways—by stimulating commercial development of farmland, promoting rural sprawl and often neglecting opportunities to build on unique local attributes—in the name of seeking to establish a "diverse economic base." By diversity, it should be noted, we often mean making one rural area just like another. The challenge, then, is whether federal agencies can be made more sensitive to the need to preserve the historic, cultural and natural resources of our rural areas and small towns in ways that will foster their economic vitality.

The Economic Development Administration of the U.S. Department of Commerce, in trying to meet the economic concerns of our smaller cities and rural communities, could, I believe, oversee and assure the protection of the historic and cultural amenities that are unique to those areas. The Community Development Block Grant Program, administered by the U.S. Department of Housing and Urban Development, could help provide an economic base that will permit the protection and wise use of the resources that are our heritage. The national park program and the Land and Water Conservation Fund grants to the states could protect the attributes of small towns and historic landscapes as vital economic elements of our nation. These are among the hopeful program opportunities the federal government can exploit.

The migration of jobs and people from the older cities and fiscal distress in some cities have caused neglect of our historic urban parks, as well as loss of investment vital to support historic neighborhoods. President Carter's proposed urban recreation program would help to maintain the parks and recreation services neglected because of higher priorities. Other federal aid programs, like HUD's Urban Development Action Grant program, are intended quickly to stimulate private investment in central-city resources. Often these grants will affect historic districts, and whether these federal leverage projects reflect the appropriate scale, whether they will be sensitive to existing neighborhood structures and to the fostering of diverse urban cultures needs to have careful attention.

Particularly interesting to watch will be the so-called gentrification of urban areas. It is unclear whether this trend is, or will become, as statistically significant as it is in Washington, D.C., or Baltimore. If so, then while we can applaud the reinvestment in historic districts, we must respond to problems of urban dislocation. Preservationists do not need more of an "elitist" image. We should promote social diversity to match the desired diversity of our built environment.

Major Problems to Address
In the face of these rural and urban trends, there are some major problems for us to work on.

First, federal responses to rural and urban development reflect no clear and concerted national policy toward historic preservation. Integration of historical and cultural values with rural landscape and the built environment is—and will continue to be—only painfully achieved. It is fortunate that our federal programs must review their impact on our national heritage, but that is only a modest check on traditional federal program goals.

Second, no federal agency today is a clear and constant advocate of community cohesion and historic preservation in our cities and towns, although the U.S. Department of the Interior might someday play that role.

Third, we cannot expect that federal funding for state and local programs, as well as direct federal historic preservation and rehabilitation programs—now at some $150 million—will ever become a large and significant part of the national budget.

Each of these problems simply reinforces the need for preservation organizations to do their utmost to watch over federal programs. Our public works programs, especially, need watching. We need to work toward developing a broad and openly arrived at national historic preservation policy, incorporating all federal agencies' programs.

In the last several years, we have seen heartening efforts to develop a broad historic preservation policy, one that emphasizes the relationships of historic preservation to social and economic needs of rural and urban communities. The National Heritage Program, recently submitted to Congress by the administration, is rightly intended to respond to the need for federal program links between cultural, historic and natural preservation needs. It would help the states establish needed inventories of natural and historic areas needing protection. In addition, it would establish a new federal government natural area register to be integrated into an overall heritage protection program.

Roles for Preservationists

Preservation efforts must not, of course, be confined to Washington's bureaucracy. Private, nonprofit organizations can supply intellectual energy, financial support and administrative coordination in supporting new directions in historic preservation throughout the nation. Their flexibility, money, clout, freedom and ideas are critical to push new programs and, in a sense, to create new public initiatives.

Two directions are of special interest.

In urban preservation and conservation, we need to stabilize neighborhoods in order to prevent displacement and to keep real estate prices at levels that will enable people of different incomes to live in rehabilitated communities. The traditional revolving fund has allowed organizations to buy commercial buildings, fix them up and sell them at a profit. Now they must recognize that all properties need not be sold at a profit; some properties must have lower prices. It may be easier to fix up property and rent it, as has been done in Pittsburgh. In such cases, organizations may have to interfere in the marketplace to prevent displacement.

Most preservation groups have concentrated their efforts in residential areas. However, rising real estate prices in commercial areas or rehabilitated neighborhoods have forced out most of the small-scale and service activities, leaving those areas open to franchises and tourist-oriented facilities. By buying commercial buildings and renting out space, private preservation organizations can prevent the disappearance of service establishments and the escalation of real estate values to the extent that the social fabric of the community is altered.

In both these situations, private, nonprofit groups have the opportunity, through revolving funds and other techniques, to assure social goals of providing urban neighborhoods with mixed incomes and mixed economic-social opportunities.

In rural preservation and conservation, private, nonprofit organizations should follow a smiliar course. It will be particularly important to pull together the land conservation and historic preservation interests that now often go in separate directions. Rural preservation requires concern, not just for land acquisition and housing and building rehabilitation, but also for the health of existing rural communities. Just as with cities, rural areas increasingly will suffer from price escalation and displacement.

There is a particular need to protect rural communities and landscapes that have unique and complex ecological, cultural and recreational qualities and a definable sense of place. The national or state park models simply cannot apply to these "living" landscapes. An especially promising concept designed to protect these unique areas is that of the "Greenline Park." Under that scheme, an area would be delineated and managed by a local or regional body that would acquire only the most critical resources. Through easements, zoning and other regulatory techniques, it would seek to protect the natural and cultural values of the area and its economic and social vitality.

This concept has been applied in the Adirondacks, which is 65 percent privately owned, and is now being tried in the

Pine Barrens of New Jersey, where Congress recently authorized establishment of a Pinelands National Reserve, covering 900,000 acres. The reserve includes towns and rural areas with unique ecological, cultural and historic attributes. Federal involvement will be simply to approve a regional plan and give front-end money for the acquisition of critical resource areas.

During the next decade, there is, I believe, good reason to hope that the preservation movement will successfully broaden its scope and apply a variety of new techniques to help achieve the goal I quoted earlier—"to preserve important historic, cultural and natural aspects of our national heritage and maintain, wherever possible, an environment which supports diversity and variety of individual choice." Awareness of the opportunity and the need to build on our national heritage is strong within our changing urban and rural areas. Let us trust that we have reason to be optimistic.

PERSPECTIVE ON PRESERVATION

Michael Middleton

The very first sentence of the report of the 1967 preservation conference at Williamsburg states, "Preservation is now recognized as only a part of a wider concern for the conservation of all natural and cultural resources, and for the enhancement of the total environment." Not bad for 13 years ago.

There is no need to debate this proposition now; other policy documents in the United States and all the instruments of the great international organizations have stressed that integrated conservation must relate to the imperatives of economic, social and land-use planning.

Conservation is an area of overlapping concern, a meeting point to which a whole range of specialists bring their expertise. This view in no way diminishes its importance. Nor does it negate the need for a more coherent philosophy of conservation, because the preservation-conservation concept is not a simple one. For some it can mean the retention of a structure's original fabric, unchanged, unrestored, until it falls down. For other people it means the replacement of defective elements and the rebuilding of ruins (even if this is based on sheer imagination); moving buildings to new sites; introducing adaptive uses; protecting street patterns and urban spaces, even though the buildings forming the spaces may have changed; conserving character; improving and enhancing areas and urban waste lots with judicious, modern infill; removing wires and outdoor advertising; landscaping and traffic management; etc.

And motivations are no less varied. They include historicism, pure and simple; aesthetic, social, economic values; education; cultural tourism; the demands of national and local identity (think of the rebuilding of Warsaw, for instance); and energy and resource conservation.

These objectives are not necessarily compatible. We have to make quite difficult trade-offs. To recycle a building must

Michael Middleton is executive director, Civic Trust, London, England.

destroy its validity as a historical document. The use of empty cottages in an English village for weekend and holiday homes may be the only way to save them, but to the sociologists the passing of the traditional village way of life will be deplored.

The Dangers of Success

Moving to the larger canvas of the protected area, we seek to interest a wider segment of the public in their heritage. But suppose we succeed! In at least one English cathedral city, sizable areas of nice old housing have been cleared to provide parking space for tourists. In others, office accommodation and new shopping centers have been built behind the original facades, and the historic image has been conserved only as theater scenery. At what point does conservation at this level fall into the make-believe world of Disneyland? There are no rules of thumb in these matters, which is why we have to be clear as to exactly what we are trying to achieve in every case, all the while remembering that every asset we let go is gone forever.

We have to remain open-minded and avoid self-imprisonment within any particular mental set. This presents two dangers. The first is the temptation to fight old battles over again. The problems of the Vieux Carré 30 years ago, for example, arose from a sluggish local economy; the area was in decay. The problem with the Vieux Carré today arises from the high economic pressures engendered by tourism and allied factors—pressures to redevelop more profitably and to insert a more comprehensive service infrastructure. Same area, but a different problem.

The second danger, which is the other side of the same coin, is the hypnotic effect on all of us of the pendulum swing of fashion. Almost by definition, the preferred solution, the accepted wisdom of 15 years ago, is now the unforgivable sin. For example, large-scale clearance programs are totally discredited, but could it be that the present enthusiasm for conservation will, in turn, be put aside in favor of some new novelty? There are certainly signs in Britain of a possible backlash against the more extreme preservation ethic. Warning signals of this kind should cause the private sector to approach its conservation programs

71

with rigor and discipline, with a determination to take the long and objective, and perhaps the unfashionable, view.

Politicians, for reasons best known to themselves, always hope to be reelected in three or four years' time, and so this period represents the limit of their thinking. But crash programs and major environmental surgery tend to be crude in relation to the delicately balanced organism of a living community, and the range of uncertainties in any system of forecasting is always greater than is publicly admitted.

So far as may be possible, we should seek to approximate the slower, steadier, more organic processes of change that shaped our settlements in the past. We should minimize our interventions in historic areas, if only to leave the maximum flexibility of choice to future generations, whose needs certainly will not be the same as ours. We can all agree on this in relation to redevelopment and renewal; but it has a bearing, too, on our approach to conservation. So far, for understandable reasons, we have had to be concerned largely with finite emergency rescue operations. Now we must learn to see conservation as a continuing process and concern ourselves with the day-to-day procedures and methodologies necessary to maintain our historic areas in good health, so that great rescue operations will not be necessary. Prevention is not only better than cure but much, much cheaper. The Main Street program of the National Trust is marvelous, but the real breakthrough will be when the Main Street programs as such are no longer necessary. We need to evolve a new kind of urban estate management, on a city scale, and in this context long-term policies are more likely to serve our ends than short-term programs. This will demand new attitudes, new patterns of administration and procedure. It implies better coordination of government departments; new consortium arrangements by official and unofficial agencies—business, industry, the professions, property owners; and bringing conservation into alignment with the normal market forces.

Conservation: A Matter of Necessity

When all concerned address themselves as specialists to the values of conservation as a matter of necessity and routine, our problems of today will cease to exist. In working toward this goal, the private sector has a crucial role to play. We are the antennae of society. We have a vision; we proclaim it to the larger community; and, when the community has absorbed it, there is a call for requisite action through legislation and official channels. At this point our role changes. We need to draw attention no longer to what needs doing, but rather to how it should be done—how, for example, to ensure, within a framework of permissive legislation and delegated executive powers, minimum performance standards.

So, what should be our guidelines as we look forward into the 1980s? First, conservation has few absolutes. Let us respect the views of others, even when they are not totally in line with our own. We must seek common ground wherever possible with politicians and developers, of course, but among ourselves, no less. And let us seek to build consortia of interests around agreed-on objectives.

Second, we must be crystal clear as to what those objectives are and the nature of the trade-offs associated with them. Let us try always to take account of the second and third-order effects of our decisions, something we have not been terribly good at in the past; these effects may become apparent only in 10 or 20 years' time. Be cautious. When in doubt, leave the options open for future generations.

Third, we should cultivate the tenacity to sustain programs over long periods. We must apply dedication and drive to establishing the methodologies required for the continuing day-to-day management and enhancement of our heritage, to assure that our cities and historic places are handed on to our children enriched and more beautiful than when we received them.

To make any impact in this world, we have to be hard and realistic, with our feet firmly on the ground. At times we all become frustrated and despondent, but we must never doubt that the work in which we are engaged is crucial to the future of the society in which we live.

Ulysses, home from Troy, exclaimed that, having seen the cities of men, he knew their minds. But although we shape our surroundings, they do, at the same time, in some measure, shape us. In seeking to preserve and enrich whatever is of quality in our surroundings now, we are helping

73

to design the nature and values of civilized society in the future. That is the magnitude of the challenge we face.

WAKING UP THE PRIVATE SECTOR

Patrick J. Leahy

We are at this conference because we share one belief: It is the knowledge and preservation of our nation's past that gives dimension to the present and direction to the future. We believe that the dreams of the future are built on the history of the past.

Until recently, many people have thought that the main goal of the historic preservation movement has been only to provide a brass plaque for every one of the more than 1,000 beds in which George Washington allegedly managed to sleep. Until recently, historic preservation has meant nothing more to people than the restoration of individual monuments, the rehabilitation of historic landmarks, battlefields and homes associated with figures or events of national importance.

In the past, local officials and city planners, unaware of the advantages and economic potential of historic preservation and possessed by an "edifice complex," chose to construct new buildings rather than restore old, familiar ones. The tearing down of historic buildings often resulted in the breaking down of local community pride and integrity.

Today it is a well-known fact that historic preservation projects are much more labor intensive and cost effective than new construction. An analysis by the Advisory Council on Historic Preservation of the projects funded under the Economic Development Act has shown that while demolition and new construction yielded an average of 70 jobs per $1 million expended, renovation—including historic preservation—created 109 jobs per $1 million expended. Restoration results in almost twice as many economic opportunities as new construction.

Furthermore, restoration also conserves raw materials consumed by new construction, and the energy needs are often far less during both the restoration process and the

Patrick J. Leahy is a U.S. senator from Vermont.

subsequent operation of the structure.

Challenging Awareness

The federal government is coming to terms with the realization that if we do not stop and take a long, sober look before we demolish our past, then its role as providers for the future is based on a shallow understanding of where we came from and where we are headed. A great deal of progress has been made at the national level to assure that federal grant programs make special considerations for the reuse of historic structures in lieu of new construction.

However, the federal government can provide only the impetus for the preservation movement. It is the beneficiaries or the private sector that must come forward and meet the challenge. For it is only through the public's awareness and the financial support of the local communities that they will be able to say to the federal government, "We challenge you." It is the responsibility of all of us to stimulate the public's interest and to educate private business on the economic benefits of historic preservation.

Some examples of how federal grant programs can inspire private investment and at the same time create new jobs and revitalize downtown areas are occurring in my home state of Vermont. The city of Winooski has received preliminary application approval from the U.S. Department of Housing and Urban Development for an Urban Development Action Grant of $1.6 million. The funds will be structured as a loan to the developer of a historic woolen mill, which will be rehabilitated into 150 rental units and 22,000 square feet of commercial space. The private financial commitment totals $4.6 million. That amounts to three private dollars for every one federal dollar. And, in addition, 50 new permanent jobs will be created.

In the second largest city in Vermont, Rutland, a historic preservation project to revitalize the downtown area resulted in the creation of 60 permanent jobs. The federal investment in this project was $350,000. Were there 50 individuals on welfare or unemployment compensation, the cost to the federal government would have been $360,000 annually.

These are just two examples of how cooperation between

76

the public and private sectors can provide an important link in preserving the past for the future.

Persuading Congress

Despite the proven promise of historic preservation, Congress has appropriated the full authorized amount for historic preservation only twice since 1966. In fiscal year 1977, despite a backlog of $300 million in preservation project requests, only $17.5 million was appropriated. Citing that backlog, I was able to persuade my colleagues on the Senate Appropriations Committee and in the full Senate to set the spending level for fiscal year 1978 at $80 million, nearly a fivefold increase over the previous year. Unfortunately, the House of Representatives would accept only $45 million for historic preservation. In the 1979 fiscal year we were more successful; $60 million was appropriated for the program. Incidentally, the Senate-passed figure was the fully authorized $100 million.

However, in order for Congress to take heed of those who say that the current level of funding is insufficient—I say to them, Where is your community support? Provide me with proof that your commitment is at least as solid as that of the federal government. Show me sound financial support from the private sector and then take your case to the Hill.

We in Congress are finding it increasingly difficult to justify and fight for adequate budgets in the midst of a national outcry for a balanced federal budget. If we are to be at all successful in our efforts to provide adequate funding for preservation, then the thrust must come from the private sector. It is these people who hold the key to the future of the preservation movement.

Fiscal Conservatism

In this time of fiscal conservatism, only the best, most cost-effective and well-administered programs will survive.

It is my hope that the importance of conserving and preserving our rich national heritage will not be overlooked in the movement to conserve federal resources. It is my belief that historic preservation is a fiscally responsible program and a sound investment in the future of our country.

It has been said that the only thing we learn from history is that we do not learn. I wholeheartedly disagree with that.

We can and must learn the value of historic preservation to our communities—to our nation. For a nation that is not conscious of its own past, there can be no link to the future.

PART 3:

FUTURE DIRECTIONS
SYMPOSIA PAPERS

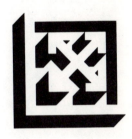

INTRODUCTION

In 1977 the Board of Trustees of the National Trust for Historic Preservation requested a review of the recent accomplishments, present status and future directions of the preservation efforts of the private sector in the United States. The vehicle selected to begin this process was the National Trust 1978 Annual Meeting and Preservation Conference held in Chicago. Five symposia, entitled "Future Directions," were planned as a part of that program. Overall responsibility for the development of the symposia was the task of a special committee on the National Preservation Conference (see page 11), which worked with National Trust staff. Fifteen speakers were invited to address specific topics suggested by the committee. Each symposium included commentators, panel discussion and audience questions.

The results of the Chicago symposia were utilized in establishing the agenda and providing a background for the smaller Williamsburg conference held in March 1979, the intent of which was to chart more specifically the future directions of the private sector in the American preservation effort.

Each speaker at the Chicago meeting was provided in advance with a general outline of all the topics the committee wished to have discussed. Not all of the speakers adhered to the committee's request concerning the scope and treatment of their topics. All of the papers are included here as presented; the authors were afforded the opportunity of post-conference editorial review. The comments made during the discussion period of each symposium have been summarized.

A LOCAL PERSPECTIVE
Arthur P. Ziegler, Jr.

The sources of revenue for preservation are changing and broadening; so, too, is our role in preserving the buildings and neighborhoods of the United States. In this time of transition, there are many things from which we might take heart and also learn.

The first is that you don't have to look very far to see that preservation is becoming a permanent, integrated institution. When I go to a city nowadays, for example, it is not necessary to ask, Do you have a preservation group? Instead, one asks, Where is the preservation group? With legislation on the local level, the question is not, Do you have a preservation ordinance? It is, What are the provisions of your ordinance?

Government's New Interest

Government agencies are more interested in preservation. The U.S. Department of Housing and Urban Development says a great deal these days about rehabilitation and conservation if not about restoration. Even the U.S. General Services Administration is attempting to redeem itself by leasing space in historic buildings rather than in modern buildings, provided they offer equal facilities. Those are remarkable developments and there are others. Universities now award degrees in preservation and planning; the National Historic Preservation Fund is now established to channel funds from offshore drilling into conservation and preservation, assuring us that money will roll in.

Some major developments serve as a pointer to the future. The first is the broad-scale interest in preservation at every level of government and that, in turn, means not only laws but money. Besides the new trust fund, there is also the Tax Reform Act of 1976—perhaps the most important thing that has happened to preservation at the federal level since 1966, when the National Historic Preservation Act was passed.

Arthur P. Ziegler, Jr., is president, Pittsburgh History and Landmarks Foundation and Landmarks Planning, Inc., Pittsburgh, Pa., and a trustee of the National Trust.

The tax act gave us accelerated depreciation for investment in National Register and otherwise certified historic buildings, which is changing local preservation organizations rapidly.

In looking at the sources of revenue for the last 12 months for the Pittsburgh History and Landmarks Foundation, a local organization in an urban area, I asked what government money we receive and where it comes from. I was amazed to learn how many different agencies our organization had approached and, miraculously, how many from which funds had been received. The obvious agency was the U.S. Department of the Interior. The funds that Interior provides are growing every year; they come to us through the states. The National Endowment for the Arts has granted us project funds; from that agency, too, we have more good prospects with its new Challenge Grant program.

Money also comes from HUD for subsidized lease and sale housing, for planning and for historic preservation. With the help of U.S. Department of Labor Comprehensive Employment and Training Act (CETA) workers, our organization did about $180,000 worth of restoration work in 10 months. We also obtained a sizable grant from the Economic Development Administration, because preservation can mean economic development, a fact only now being realized.

We also received a grant from the U.S. Department of Energy that is going to be used for the installation of solar equipment for an old warehouse being converted to an office building. Such major sources of revenue are just beginning to open up.

Channeling Private Money

Another source of funding is the National Trust, which is placing more money in its National Preservation Revolving Fund and Endangered Properties Program.

The Tax Reform Act has made an enormous amount of private money available because preservationists are now joined with the industrialists and private developers. In a 25-day period, 18 developers came from other cities to my office in Pittsburgh looking for projects involving old buildings that are listed or eligible for listing in the National Register of Historic Places. They are ready to do what our organization has been trying to do since 1964—restore downtown.

Newsletters that come from professional organizations and lobbying and special-interest groups are filled with preservation information. Real estate newsletters, journals of auditors and accountants, legal journals, shopping center newspapers all feature articles on preservation, reuse, adaptive use and tax benefits.

An Internal Revenue Service ruling now enables nonprofit preservation groups to buy and sell property. No longer do we have to masquerade as educational institutions in order to have a revolving fund to do historic district work. That is a tremendous breakthrough, and it enables us to raise money directly for projects we want to fund.

Philanthropic funds are a source of help to preservation as government takes over more and more of health, welfare and education responsibilities. Those private dollars must go somewhere. At the moment, the arts are coming in first, with preservation a good runner-up.

A wonderful thing has happened—Proposition 13, which should not be looked on as a restriction or compression of dollars. It is giving a tremendous opportunity for us to do something to help government; we must go forth to do a job efficiently. As nonprofit groups, this is the time for us to tell government, Spend your community development dollars not on yourselves but on us; we can get the job done at lower cost and faster.

It is not so much the cost of government that troubles taxpayers; it is the failure to produce a result or a product. This is something that preservationists can do, and it opens up vast sources of money. The town of Worcester, Mass., for example, gives $35,000 a year in community development money to a local preservation group, which pays half the salary of the director and provides money for a facade restoration revolving fund.

Other things working in preservationists' favor are energy conservation and inflation, because our foundations are solid, our walls are up and they are stout walls that keep out the weather. Sound construction has an effect on preservation groups. Almost every city in the country has a hot real estate market today. It is no longer necessary to worry, as we did a few years ago, about who is going to live in these buildings. Now we worry about who is being displaced as new residents move in. Preservationists are going to be the catalysts to get government and private interests moving to help the inner city, and we can do this without quantities of money.

More often than not, the neighborhood conservationists are not including historic preservation in their plans, and we, in turn, are failing to include them. Preservationists must decide whether to be neighborhood organizers or to join the neighborhood movement or to give up such projects, because the neighborhood conservation movement is growing and getting its own legislation passed.

Preservationists as Developers

Preservationists are going to do something that government did at Boston's Quincy Market and the Gallery in Philadelphia—melding old and new construction. Preservationists are going to become subsidizers to bring private projects up to where the private market can take over. But it would be wise, in some instances, to include ourselves in with the developer so that we receive a share of the cash flow on projects that we help, and there is a new source of revenue for this. The city government did it at Quincy Market, did it at the Gallery—it was not just taxes that interested the government in those projects; it was actual participation in cash flow.

Preservationists may at times have to be the developers, that is, go in and raise the money, buy the buildings and develop them. We are allowed to do that. If necessary, preservationists can join with a private interest and do the job together. Pittsburgh History and Landmarks is developing the largest adaptive use project now under way in the nation, the $45 million Station Square project. It is the owner, outright, of the largest renewal project ever undertaken in the city's downtown area, and the project is doing far better than many government-funded projects in Pittsburgh.

Preservationists are also going to be, more than ever, the gadflies, the ones who say, "Don't destroy it;"—the ones who go around and say, "Okay, you want to use it, but you must use it well." Preservationists must provide the design

85

services, or at least the design guidance, to assure a project's success. They must also assure that the intent of legislative actions is actually carried out at the local level. Preservationists must promote the ideas and perhaps even go in and block demolition long enough, hold the fort long enough, for someone in the private sector to understand, come in and do the job.

Thinking Big

While I feel very optimistic, I am also worried, because we preservationists should not content ourselves with getting a little revolving fund going, publicizing the historic district and luring some people in to do the job. They tend to think small; they must think big.

Preservation has become broader and more complex in recent times. However, we have a tremendous record of success, and we accomplished that without any significant money for the past 30 years. There is a growing demand in every quarter of the country for preservation; it has reached government officials in Washington, and there is a growing demand that government expense be reduced and that the private world take over. These are all encouraging factors for the cause of preservation.

A STATE PERSPECTIVE
James A. Gray

Statewide revolving funds have given a broader geographic dimension to a highly successful technique that has been used locally in Charleston, Savannah, Pittsburgh, Annapolis and a number of other communities in the United States.

A revolving fund for historic preservation is a pool of money that is collected from one or a number of sources. The money is used to take endangered properties off the market through the acquisition of options to purchase or through outright purchase of the structures. These historic properties generally are sold to private investors. This is not to say they could not be resold to government—some are. The proceeds from such sales go back into the pool of money, which is then used over and over again to acquire additional properties.

Advantages of Revolving Funds

Local and state revolving funds are playing an increasingly significant role because they are able to move swiftly, and with a minimum of red tape—two things not all organizations, especially those in the public sector, can do. Another advantage is that the dollars in the pool are used over and over again, thus more properties can be saved. The public interest is often best served when the endangered property is put to an adaptive use, which itself contributes to the local economy. For instance, a historic warehouse in Washington, N.C., recycled by the Historic Preservation Fund of North Carolina will become a restaurant, while two large houses, one in Asheville and one in Raleigh, will become multitenant office complexes. The downtown areas of the cities where these structures are located will benefit from an infusion of people and purchasing power. A significant factor is that when endangered properties are sold to private investors they stay on the tax books, unlike a

James A. Gray was formerly executive director, Historic Preservation Fund of North Carolina, Raleigh, and is now the fund's director of development in Asheville.

historic building that is bought and turned into a nonprofit museum and is removed from the tax books.

The mechanism by which historic preservation is assured is that of restrictive covenants or protective covenants, as I prefer to call them, in the deeds with which the revolving fund agency conveys title to the purchasers of properties.

Restrictive covenants vary from city to city, situation to situation, but most of them have at least five features: (1) a requirement to restore the building in accordance with plans approved by the fund; (2) a requirement to maintain the building and its integrity; (3) a right of first refusal by the revolving fund agency upon resale of the property; (4) an option to repurchase the property, which may be exercised by the revolving fund if the covenants are violated; and (5) public access, even if it is simply to view the facade.

There are a few bonus features of statewide revolving funds. They can raise the money where the money is and save the buildings where the buildings are. This may sound a little bit like Karl Marx, but there is practical advantage to it.

In most states there are certain financial or economic centers, and if money is to be raised that is where one goes. Often, however, the finest historic buildings are in underdeveloped rural areas of the state. With a statewide revolving fund, the assets of the fund can be brought to where the needs are.

North Carolina Fund

The philosophy behind the Historic Preservation Fund of North Carolina is that it is to be used only in those areas of the state where there is little or no money, little or no interest in historic preservation and little or no historic preservation activity. The major cities that already have money, interest and preservation activity are left alone. It would be presumptuous of us to jump in on top of what is being done in Charlotte, Wilmington, Raleigh, Salisbury and other communities in the state that have active preservation programs.

Another purpose of the fund is to provide advice and encouragement to local groups and, in many cases, show them how to start their own revolving funds. This is not something that the field staff of a state's historic preservation office is likely to undertake. It has architectural historians, archeologists, architects etc., but probably no one with experience in operating a revolving fund.

A statewide revolving fund can do things for the state that the state cannot do for itself, such as buy and sell properties easily and quickly. For example, a corporation gave a fine historic property to the state of North Carolina, which accepted it with the understanding that it would not be expected to develop the property, that is, turn it into a house museum or anything like that, but probably would sell it instead.

Rather than disposing of this property, the state called on us to do it for them. Our expertise and experience were not bound by state rules, regulations and statutes concerning the sale of properties. The state gave us a six-month option at the appraised value, less 6 percent, and we are going to sell this property and put restrictive covenants on it, just as though we had acquired it from a private owner.

All revolving funds are different. Our statewide revolving fund has several unique features. While we are independent, we do work closely with everyone—including the state. Our financial support comes from a variety of sources and, perhaps most important, ours is a revolving fund and nothing else. We do not have a membership, a newsletter or education programs.

Almost exclusively we buy options, rather than properties outright, which stretches our dollars more. We obtain a six-month option on a property and then merchandise it just as though we owned it, find a buyer and have a double closing in an attorney's office. At that time we exercise our option, hold the property for perhaps one minute, turn around and reconvey it to the private investor who is also present, and our restrictive covenants are in the deed that we issue to that investor.

Use of Federal Matching Funds

We have what is perhaps a unique cooperative agreement with the state for the use of federal matching funds. It is a pass-through arrangement, a legal laundering operation, if you please, that has been approved by the Heritage Conservation and Recreation Service, U.S. Department of the Interior, our state attorney general and other officials.

In 1979 the North Carolina state historic preservation officer set aside $40,000 in federal matching funds for our use. With it we may find a property that can be bought for $80,000. We put up $40,000 and receive $40,000 from the federal matching funds; then when we resell, say for $80,000, we return 75 percent of the state's money, or $30,000, to the North Carolina treasury, earmarked for other preservation projects and completely laundered of all governmental red tape.

As a thank-you from the state, we are allowed to keep 25 percent of the $40,000, or $10,000. Federal, state and local officials are enthusiastic about this cooperative funding arrangement.

Underscoring Public Benefits

I should note two major problems that confronted us when we launched the program. First, it took 12 months and more than $6,000 in legal fees and expenses to get our tax-exempt status. We first received an unfavorable ruling from the Internal Revenue Service; then, with the help of the National Trust, the Advisory Council on Historic Preservation, the National Park Service and others, we got a favorable ruling. One difficulty was that ours was purely a revolving fund and not intended as an educational institution or anything of that sort, a fact that bothered the IRS. The unfavorable ruling said that we looked like an ordinary trade or business, engaging in real estate operations.

We appealed the ruling and were told by the IRS that it was worried about what the public benefits of our operation were. "We can see the private benefits to the person from whom you buy the property, and then the person to whom you sell the property, but where are the public benefits?" The answer to this question was provided by the National Trust, which prepared a position paper outlining the public benefits of revolving funds for historic preservation.

It became apparent to us as we reviewed our application that the IRS was especially concerned about the matter of public access. We have promised the IRS that there will be public access to our properties, but the degree of public access will depend on the nature of the property.

The second major problem to be confronted was fund raising. There is a problem in getting the initial pool of

90

money together and then replenishing the funds on a continuing basis. Our fund does have expenses—salaries, travel, telephone and office rent—that must be met. Yet over the long run we are going to sell properties for less than the normal commercial rate. Rarely will we sell property for any substantial profit. More likely, a small loss will be taken, so funds must be continually replenished to meet expenses as well as to purchase properties.

We are fortunate in that, since receiving our tax exemption in November 1977, we have raised $124,800: approximately $27,000 from three charitable foundations, $40,000 from two major North Carolina-based corporations, $800 from organizations, $7,000 from 47 individuals and $50,000 a year for two years from the North Carolina legislature.

Challenges of a Revolving Fund

There are challenges in the business of operating a revolving fund, one of which is selecting the right properties for acquisition. I ask four questions, and the answer must be "yes" to each before I am interested in a property: (1) Is the property really endangered, or does somebody live in the house and just want us to sell it for them? (2) Is it really worth saving compared with other historic properties? (3) Can it be bought at anything close to a reasonable price? (4) Is there a market for it to be resold? There is also a question in selecting the right buyer; sometimes there will be more than one who is willing and eager to purchase a property at the asking price. The questions to be asked then are: Which of the two buyers will do the best job of preservation and restoration, and which will put the property to the best use?

By its very name, a revolving fund implies that you are going to get in and out and do not want to build an inventory of real estate. It is a sound mechanism for acquiring and preserving for the public benefit a historic asset that otherwise would be lost.

A NATIONAL PERSPECTIVE
Donald Dworsky

The future of historic preservation economics flows directly from past trends and present policies. A brief description, therefore, of those trends and policies is helpful.

The first period extended from the settlement of the country to the era of industrialization, a time when growth stemmed from the apparently infinite supply of resources that America had to offer. With an emphasis on the use of these resources, the country's theme was "newness." There was no positive preservation policy.

The second period, from about 1880 until the 1920s, saw the birth of a preservation ethic in the actions of individual philanthropists and in occasional preservation actions by the federal government. This period culminated in the enactment of the Antiquities Act of 1906, which authorized the President to designate protection for specific archeological sites, and the creation in 1916 of the National Park Service to protect individual historic sites. During this period general economic conditions affected the nation's built environment through such factors as urbanization, the location of industry and the results of industrial pollution.

In the third period, from the 1920s to World War II, the role of the federal government increased with the enactment of the Historic Sites Act in 1935. This act gave the Secretary of the Interior the authority to create a comprehensive historic preservation program. The Survey of Historic Sites and Buildings began, and specialized programs such as the Historic American Buildings Survey and Historic American Engineering Record flowed out of this authority. Preservation funding still benefited individual buildings and sites, but the historic sites survey began to consider our entire patrimony. The general economic conditions of the era also contributed to interest in the reuse of natural resources as second and third generation urban dwellers became more

Donald Dworsky is the budget examiner for federal preservation programs, U.S. Office of Management and Budget, Washington, D.C.

aware of the built environment.

The fourth period, extending from the end of World War II to about 1970, saw the substantial expansion of both the direction and nature of preservation policy and economics. The success of the National Trust, the enactment of the National Historic Preservation Act of 1966, and the general economic conditions led to an expanded National Register of Historic Places. A new concept in law was that places of local, state and regional significance were also considered to be nationally significant historic properties. That is, preservation policy defined "significance" not only as properties important to the nation as a whole, but important to all Americans in their everyday life. Together, all such places comprise our national heritage. In addition, historic preservation grants were created to stimulate private and state expenditures for historic preservation, to establish programs in each state and to assist states in the survey and inventory of historic properties. A higher standard of historic preservation responsibility was assigned to federal agencies, and their actions became subject to a review by the Advisory Council on Historic Preservation.

The preservation policy of this era also was influenced by the general economics of the period. The postwar construction boom, the veterans loan program, the development of the interstate highway system and the growth of suburbs, as well as the more recent urban renewal and slum clearance programs, influenced the general policy and economics of preservation by accentuating the new, neglecting the central cities and stimulating sprawl.

Period of Great Change

These economic trends influenced and gave birth to the fifth and current period in which the focus of preservation has broadened to include historic districts and the natural settings of buildings. Instead of preserving isolated historic properties as museums, adaptive use has become a goal. Entire urban areas and whole neighborhoods are now emphasized as the focus of preservation. Preservation economics also have developed further. The historic preservation grants became a larger National Historic Preservation Fund. Even larger federal funding sources were directed to benefit the built environment, such as U.S. Department of Housing and Urban Development and U.S. Department of Commerce Economic Development Administration programs. Finally, tax incentives were enacted to help change the basic market conditions that affect historic properties. And in reaction to the alienation in the urban environment and the need for community, people have become more active in neighborhood preservation organizations. As adaptive use is shown to be profitable, local lending institutions have entered the scene as powerful actors in the economics of preservation. The most recent economic conditions—inflation and high fuel and transportation costs—also are influencing the direction of preservation policy to emphasize urban and neighborhood revitalization.

We are in a period of great change. As market and economic conditions change and as federal programs are increasingly managed to be sensitive to preservation, a changed federal role may be called for. But the federal role may be unimportant; if the focus, means and public interest in preservation continue to expand from the specific and narrow to the general and the broad, the future of historic preservation and its economics is promising, regardless of federal direct support.

The Changing Federal Role

A brief examination of the role of the federal government provides evidence that we are, indeed, moving toward a broad preservation ethic that may result in less direct federal support for preservation. Usually the federal government intervenes in market activities only when: the existing market conditions lead to a misallocation of resources or unnecessary waste; there is market failure; and there are public goods to be produced that the market is incapable of producing. These three circumstances have justified a federal role in historic preservation but, at the same time, raise several questions: What should the federal role be vis-a-vis the workings of the market? What are the best intervention strategies, the most efficient tools and effective techniques? What should be the limits to the federal role, and what should be the defining features of a preservation policy? Who, exactly, should benefit from the policy? For example, the best federal strategy would be to halt the underlying economic causes of the loss of historic resources rather than addressing symptoms. To do this, however, requires that we know what these underlying causes are, e.g., transportation technology, the amount of new construction, population growth or a traditional bias against reusing resources.

If we cannot accurately pinpoint the causes of the loss of patrimony, how can we measure the effectiveness of our preservation policy? How can we even determine the tactics of that policy? What effect has our policy had on arresting the underlying economic causes of the loss of our patrimony? We do not know the answer. Because the federal government does make expenditures for preservation, there must be some sort of policy toward preservation. But this policy exists in the absence of an analytical thought process to determine the best federal role. This lack of information can be attributed to the failure of policymakers to determine rigorously the best federal role and to the failures of program managers to conduct evaluations following program completions.

This lack of information makes it difficult to justify the federal expenditure of preservation-specific dollars, particularly since historic preservation programs must compete for funds against programs that can more specifically justify their budgets. This lack of information, too, raises continual questions about the federal investment strategy. It means that preservation policy is made in a vacuum, that policies are not as sharply defined as they could be and that preservation is probably not a concern of policymakers who design programs that do contribute to the loss of historic resources.*

The current federal preservation policy, therefore, is a mixture of laws, techniques, tools, tactics, responsibilities

*Update: Before making fiscal 1981 decisions regarding the amount and purpose of the direct federal expenditures to benefit preservation, policymakers did take into consideration other federal sums that could be used to benefit preservation by affecting the underlying economic causes of the loss of historic resources, and analyzed the effect on the market that tax expenditures for preservation have made. The result was to recommend a substantially lower direct expenditure because the market appeared to be producing the preservation benefits previously sought through direct federal expenditures.—D.D.

and activities of all different economic sectors and levels of government. This policy, created in part because we do not know the intervention technique that would benefit historic preservation most, is so diffuse that the information problem is compounded; it is even more difficult to measure the effects of our policy, to map out new directions for it and to determine the appropriate amount of funds that should be spent on preservation each year. Yet, we forge ahead and spend more than $200 million annually in pursuit of our preservation goals. Unless these questions are addressed, federal program funds will be increasingly difficult to justify as available budgetary resources become scarce, despite increasing public perceptions of the importance of preservation.

The national preservation policy has been one of increasingly large focus, expanding from individual buildings to districts and neighborhoods and from nationally significant structures to places of importance to localities. The nature of our policy has gone from preservation to adaptive use. The means of our policy have expanded from preservation-specific dollars to broader sources increasingly aimed at market conditions and the underlying causes of the loss of our heritage. The general economic conditions of our times—inflation and increased fuel and transportation costs—are further stimulating interest in the reuse of our built environment. Local lending institutions have come to realize that preservation is profitable.

This history of an ever-broadening of preservation policy into aspects of our lives that we have not directly related to preservation in the past denotes an emerging ethic in which preservation is considered in many different arenas. As this ethic becomes increasingly woven into the fabric of our day-to-day activities, preservation is assured of a favorable future even though the federal role may change to reflect these changed economic and ethical views of preservation.

DISCUSSION
Summary of comments made by panelists, audience and the commentators

Generating Support

Preservationists have been talking to themselves for a long time; they have a problem in reaching major private sector developers, bankers, lenders and donors who control funds that could be used to support preservation. As public funding for preservation increases, we may expect a closer examination by policymakers of the bases and justification for the allocation of these public funds.

Finding and maintaining preservation funding requires more than platitudes; it requires an educational effort, much work, a great deal of time and sophisticated lobbying. For local groups the use of public funds is too often marked by time-consuming reviews and reimbursement procedures.

The economic issue confronting preservationists in the 1980s is not historic preservation, reconstruction, rehabilitation or adaptive use, but rather continuing use. Our society needs to continue to use the good buildings that have been built for the purposes for which they were built.

Developing New Tax Incentives

The preservation movement is only beginning to absorb the new accelerated depreciation incentive in the federal tax code; the word is only now beginning to reach the private investment community. We really do not know how well it will work in saving buildings. A time of evaluation is needed before concluding that more incentives should be sought. The primary problem with the current federal preservation tax incentives is the amount of time it takes to have a building listed in the National Register of Historic Places and have it duly certified.

Legislative Initiatives

Historic preservation legislation should be developed carefully, especially at the local level. Ordinances should not be used to force people, such as neighborhood residents, to do what they do not want to do. It is preferable to work with them first and convince them of the need for preservation. If this is not done, preservation laws may create serious problems and hostility.

The federal government has a long way to go before the policies that Congress placed in the National Historic Preservation Act of 1966 and those the president placed in Executive Order 11593 are taken seriously and implemented by all federal agencies. We should insist that the federal government, when licensing and funding projects, assure that the historical dimension is included with imagination and enthusiasm in the planning of federal and federally funded projects. A multiplicity of federal laws would not be needed if those now on the books were properly implemented.

The Preservationist and the Developer

Preservationists must get into conversations early with developers and political authorities, so that we really do participate in total planning rather than waiting until some adverse project is proposed and only then viewing it with alarm. Neighborhoods especially should be emphasized in urban planning.

One of the major unanswered issues left is that of the role of the private developer. How do we as citizens (1) identify important urban and rural areas, (2) decide what is important about those areas, and (3) decide what can be changed or saved when developers work in such areas? How do we persuade the developers to identify what is special about the place? What is it that we can tell them when they identify what will be destroyed? What can we say that will persuade them that saving an older structure will add more to the value of a development than destroying an older structure? There is not enough money from public sources or private financial institutions to jack up otherwise noneconomic continued use of all older structures.

All cities are different. The differences may not be anything as specific as a building, a street pattern or a use, but they may be all these special pieces of the fabric woven together. If developers are going to have successful projects they should understand how these differences operate and turn them into a value. The essence of preservationists' work is to identify and protect special character while persuading developers to keep older structures for their value. All areas can continue to be special and recognizable places, no matter whether public or private funds are used.

Chicago, for example, even though it is destroying buildings, does retain a certain power that is instantly recognizable. The city where the modern skyscraper was invented has to save these significant buildings. Yet, Chicago is also continuing to grow and be itself by building internationally recognized modern skyscrapers.

Federal Preservation Funds: Magnitude and Effectiveness

The preservation funds that are currently appropriated appear to be used effectively. At issue is the magnitude of funds that are requested. Are sufficient funds available for federal agencies to inventory all their lands for historic properties and gear preservation considerations into their planning? Federal funds are always going to be limited for preservation because preservation is not the number-one priority for federal agencies. The best way to influence the use of federal funds for preservation is to be involved with the preservation ethic, to be involved with the local community when zoning decisions are made, when variances are granted, when construction projects are being designed. It is desirable that preservation disappear as a separate and special subject. If it could be institutionalized, preservation would not have to be applied so often at the end of the planning process or forced on federal agencies that have many other—to them—seemingly more important functions. Preservation as a factor for consideration should come at the beginning of the planning process, including every local decision that is made regarding historic properties and every private banking and investment decision that is faced.

The real question is whether the federal funds that are available are being used effectively, not the magnitude of additional federal dollars. The only way these funds can be made effective is for preservationists to provide input to the government to have them used wisely.

A LOCAL PERSPECTIVE
Barbara Sudler

Historic Denver is a private, nonprofit corporation organized eight years ago in response to a crisis. The crisis did not represent imminent loss of the most significant or best piece of Denver architecture, but rather the loss of a typical 1890s residence associated with a colorful Denver character, Molly Brown. Historic Denver was successful in that rescue mission, and the next cause célèbre, an attempt to save the Moffat Mansion, a superb residence dominating the edge of Capitol Hill, was a loss out of which at least two plusses developed: (1) It generated publicity and publicity generated new members; and (2) when rescue of the mansion was placed on a local referendum ballot and subsequently lost, Historic Denver still could say, "But more than 42,000 people in the Denver community cared enough to vote for the city to save the structure." From that 1972 crisis to the present, Historic Denver has won some and lost some, but our future lies in the numbers of members generated by publicity almost as much as by doing a job for which the Denver community experiences pride or pleasure.

Educational Objectives

The future objectives of Historic Denver are primarily educational; indeed, that was the thrust of our response to the U.S. Secretary of the Interior's request for broadly based input into a national preservation policy. Education and more education. We view our present and future leadership role rather as a parental one, for when we have done a good job our organization will no longer be needed. This is not to say that Denver can do without us yet, but rather that there is nothing wrong with looking ahead and defining what there is between here and successful completion of the task. We believe educational objectives are best accomplished by the private sector, for the formalized bureaucracy

Barbara Sudler was executive administrator, Historic Denver, Denver, Colo., at the time these remarks were delivered and is now executive director of the Colorado Historical Society.

too easily slips into jargon, which simply is not listened to by most of those we want to reach. The educational objective of Historic Denver is met in a number of ways: a monthly newspaper (good enough that we do not like to call it a newsletter); taking advantage of every opportunity to speak to diverse groups; promoting things such as the historic preservation supplement to the *Denver Post;* testifying when asked to, even on losing propositions, for doing so provides an opportunity to educate.

Publications provide another educational opportunity. We budgeted $10,000 in the 1979 fiscal year for publications, most of which will fund a book on the historic and architectural background of an inner-city area within which we operate a revolving fund. Every penny spent on the monthly newspaper can be thought of as an educational expense, some $8,000 during the year, with another $2,500 for the part-time editor's salary.

The Challenge of Projects Ignored by Others

In addition to the present and future educational role of the private nonprofit organization, we see challenge and opportunity in projects ignored by others. For example, the 9th Street Historic Park was an adaptive use project that only Historic Denver was willing to assume; upon completion it became a strikingly successful metaphor for neighborhood revitalization. Actually, our revolving fund work in an inner-city neighborhood is in many ways built on the success of saving 9th Street, a million-dollar project. Not only did that project achieve a tremendously important preservation goal, but it also built a foundation for the next project and gave our organization credibility. We intend to continue to fill the gap that the public sector leaves, for Denver has a city administration not always readily responsive to our goals and an urban renewal authority that often maintains the traditional monolithic profile.

We use the gap between the public sector's reluctance and our energetic acceptance of the project as another educational opportunity, and we use it in a positive way. We at Historic Denver believe that the "kamikaze pilot" days of historic preservation are gone. That quixotic pilot was willing to die to accomplish the assignment; we operate on the notion that winning is everything and winning implies staying alive. Therefore, each project is owed as much planning as we can give it, and in this connection we recognize that planning in the face of a gap between the public and private sectors is immensely difficult to accomplish. But our organizational structure helps us to perform in the face of a heady dichotomy.

Other Opportunities

Further educational opportunities we make for ourselves. We spent some months trying to expand our readership's understanding of such issues as infill housing by developing guidelines for their consideration drawn from all over the country. Infill we consider to be one of the huge issues of the future, and we ask ourselves what truly will have been won by historic district status if deleterious infill all but wipes out the impact of the treasured structures.

While infill is of vital importance, we work on smaller amenities as we go along—fences, landscaping, porch detailing. We hope to publish a series of pamphlets on these subjects that will be serviceable to all areas of the city, not just historic districts.

As the neighborhood movement grows in America, we see the same burgeoning power in Denver that exists elsewhere. In Denver the movement is as yet a paper tiger, but we think great political clout lies within the germinating process, a time when citizens learn that power exists in numbers. We hope that Historic Denver, a citywide, indeed metropolitan areawide, movement, can effect through these neighborhood groups downzoning as required by certain residential districts in order to bring them back to first-class condition. Thus, coordination of groups with different geographies and constituencies but mutual goals is a future role. We hope we can endow these diverse groups with a sibling attitude toward one another. Then, when one neighborhood is threatened by an unfortunate incursion, other, unthreatened neighborhoods would testify on behalf of the affected one.

Defining Objectives

It is natural to concern ourselves with process as we develop a list of objectives. How does Historic Denver determine an objective? The final responsibility rests with the Board of Trustees and, while its votes are often subjective, we try to achieve objectivity. Every project of Historic Denver is run by an advisory committee with a trustee chairing that body. Chairpersons of major projects are on the executive committee of the Board of Trustees, which meets every Monday afternoon to review all projects. Most advisory committees have a staff liaison person. (Historic Denver has eight staff members who cover nine specific areas.) Each advisory committee meets at least monthly and usually twice a month, with the staff liaison in attendance.

No matter how much we wish that it were the old days when volunteers did all the work, it is not and staff is, in the final analysis, whom you can count on. There are times, however, when we lean heavily on volunteers, such as the 500 who work each night of the four-night fund-raising event, "A Night in Old Denver." However, in dealing with the city council, in dealing with the community development department (the city agency that administers U.S. Department of Housing and Urban Development block grants), in dealing with the state historic preservation office, in dealing with Colorado's new energy code, we need staff to present our case.

The staff advisory committee determines objectives to propose to the executive committee. The executive committee then makes either a favorable or an unfavorable recommendation to the Board of Trustees. When an objective is assumed, we know what our roles are: trustees to establish policy and direction, staff to move forward in the way chosen by the trustees.

Until the recent development of our educational model, our projects were all brick and mortar and therefore simple to assess as to success. Within our biggest current project, neighborhood revitalization, there are some goals beyond education and structural rebirth: minimum displacement, application of restrictive covenants on a significant number of properties, development of new financial tools to enhance both the work and the fund-raising prospects. We are now, for example, looking at various ways that we might acquire a facade easement from an elderly owner, leaving with that owner a life estate in the property, paying that owner on a monthly basis for our ownership of the facade with the unpaid balance going to the natural heirs at the time of the life estate owner's death. Granted that technique would only hold off displacement for one generation, but maybe it would be greedy for us to expect greater surety than that.

Bridging Public-Private Sector Gap

We also consider it appropriate as a private, nonprofit organization to bridge the gap between the private and public sectors and have successfully worked with the Colorado State Division of Housing, which seems to admire our ability to work toward goals it shares. With the exception of this one bureau, we are generally able to move a project along somewhat faster outside the bureaucracy, which is often hamstrung with regulations and fears.

Coordination of effort is of great concern to us. When we cannot find someone to fill that role, Historic Denver leaps into the breach. Somehow or other, this coordination has to be accomplished. When historic preservationists speak with one voice they are most powerful. To require uniformity all the time is unrealistic, but we do owe each other an ongoing conversation on shared interests. Such conversation does not always take place, not because of animosity or rivalry, but because we are all so busy that we simply do not take the time to update one another. Recently, the U.S. Department of the Interior's Heritage Conservation and Recreation Service (HCRS) held meetings in Denver and, although we were said to have been on the list of invitees, Historic Denver did not receive an invitation. We have administered Interior Department preservation grants-in-aid; we propose many of the Denver nominations to the National Register of Historic Places; in short, one would think that there is every reason to include Historic Denver in such an informational gathering. It is an example of one hand not knowing what the other is doing, and it is an issue that could get worse before it gets better.

If HCRS has problems getting the Denver groups together, think what a coordination problem exists among groups that do not have natural affinities. While a great deal of our city work is uphill, there is nothing harder than securing current information on what the city administration expects to do with various sectors of the city. We have, however, been successful in getting two significant 1978-79 grants: $100,000 from the U.S. Department of Housing and Urban Development block grants and $92,000 from the U.S. Department of Labor's Comprehensive Employment and Training Act. Those grants moved forward our work in Curtis Park and neighborhood revitalization, but we were unsuccessful in the next funding year in getting the neighborhood into the city's district of greatest need.

The differing elements of the private sector will not even have a chance if private enterprise does not make the adaptive use programs happen. This is happening in Denver, with Larimer Square as both leader and guide. The nonprofit sector, as demonstrated by Historic Denver, must play a strong educational role. Our staff can recite explanations of the Tax Reform Act of 1976 and yet there are still people who do not seem to know that renovation of commercial properties is now competitive with new construction. Furthermore, we need to inspire people who are beginning to share our goals to realize that there are affinity groups willing to help, advise and identify with them.

The private sector is best reached through education, legal and financial incentives and that amorphous realm of individual aspirations. One must play the game by the rules that make it interesting and easy for the newspapers: lots of personal interest stories on small successes; tours of districts and areas; people stories and rich history stories; lots of one-to-one education—take your concerns to cocktail parties!

Historic Denver owns eight facade easements and now looks toward aggressively soliciting more; this will be a lengthy educational effort. State legislation on property tax incentives exists in Colorado, but this information needs to be put before the public.

Lack of coordination makes private-public communication difficult. Historic Denver believes the private sector should take the initiative just to make sure that the gauntlet is picked up. It is our sector's responsibility to make sure that the conversation is an ongoing one, much as we would wish for someone to be the traffic officer saying whose turn it is now. The tangled world of public bureaucracies will get worse. We must learn to live with it by providing clarification. But that does not mean that we will always be on top of the information or the opportunities.

The bottom line in Denver is that for the most part the public sector considers us a nuisance, and once we are involved we are a bother with our endless questions. We try to think politically; we try to sell on the basis of what interests the buyer; we try to be diplomatic. We comment on all federally mandated A-95 review and coordination procedures, all city and state projects, all transportation issues and, when possible, we couch our remarks in helpful rather than hysterical terms. We try to bring up issues well in advance in order for preservation and heritage goals to be considered. All of us dislike being drawn up short at the 11th hour, so we try to think ahead.

What Lies Ahead?

Where are we going in the years ahead? Historic Denver is going to have to be involved in issues such as pollution, transportation, photogrammetry and to take some interesting stands to upgrade the quality of contemporary architecture. All the while we shall seek to hone our administrative act and manage our money more soundly, for the day when the nonprofit group spent with profligacy is gone; the private sector is not going to underwrite us if our management is shallow. We have to show maturity. We shall stay alive in order to improve the urban fabric and to try to make a difference in people's lives. For what we do is for people.

A STATE PERSPECTIVE
Bradley Hale

In the past few years there has been great interest in the nonprofit, statewide preservation organization. New York, Florida, Washington and Georgia are among many that have formed state groups, and other states have expressed an interest in doing so. What does this mean? After the passage of the National Historic Preservation Act of 1966 there was a tremendous growth in local historic preservation organizations. Now there is an acceleration in state groups. If we focus on the role of a state organization, such as the Georgia Trust for Historic Preservation, we see how it interplays with the roles of the national organization, the local organizations and the public sector.

Three Main Functions

Our organization has three functions, probably of equal importance: coordination, education and legislation. Coordination of local groups as a broad constituency within the state is a political function and an increasingly important one for a state organization.

In 1978 Georgia had a $200 million surplus, and state officials were concerned because of the Proposition 13 movement in California. In reaction, the Commissioner of Natural Resources reduced the allocation for historic preservation. When we learned about this action, we called representatives from Savannah, Macon, Columbus, Athens and Atlanta to meet with the commissioner to express our concern. We told him that we thought there were more than 100,000 constituents in Georgia involved in some way in preservation. That got his attention! Coordination of local groups did the job. Nobody else had the portfolio to convene these people; we were the logical ones.

We view another aspect of our coordination role as the development of a network of knowledgeable people in local areas to whom certain preservation problems can be re-

Bradley Hale is president, Georgia Trust for Historic Preservation, Atlanta, Ga.

ferred. With 159 counties we have made a statewide network a priority for 1980.

Our second function, education, is most important for us. The Georgia Trust publishes a quarterly newsletter and a pamphlet series and provides technical advice on funding and restoration problems. In addition, we sponsor conferences, one-day tours and an annual meeting.

Our third function, legislation, is viewed as a vital part of our commitment to the statewide preservation movement. We are registered lobbyists and we take positions on issues involving the governor's office or the legislature. The Georgia Trust has a legislative committee that has drafted enabling legislation for historic districts.

The Georgia Trust for Historic Preservation arose out of political concerns five years ago when then Gov. Jimmy Carter reorganized the state government. The Georgia Historical Commission was put under a larger umbrella, the state historic preservation office. Concerned people, initially led by the state historic preservation office, formed the Georgia Trust as a private constituency to be heard by the political forces in the state.

The Georgia Trust does not emphasize property stewardship, but when we were offered the Hay House in Macon, which may be the finest example of Italian Renaissance Revival architecture in the country, we took it. The house came with a $100,000 endowment; it has become tangible evidence of our presence in the state. Located in the central city of Georgia, it is convenient for our board meetings. So, while we are property owners, that is less important than our three primary functions of group coordination, education and legislation.

Several years ago, the National Trust focused on whether or not it should have state chapters. The results of a questionnaire the National Trust sent out were almost unanimously "no." I agree with this. I think it is healthy to have independent local organizations.

In the future the statewide groups will grow. They will rely on organizations such as the National Trust to monitor national legislation and court cases, for technical advice and for coordination and information among the various independent state groups—functions the National Trust could do well. The National Trust can rely on the states for grassroots political support, getting us to activate our people in dealing with Congress.

The National Trust receives 25,000 inquiries a year on preservation matters. It seems to me, although it would stretch our staff, that those inquiries that come from Georgia could be answered by our staff; the responsibility could be put back in Atlanta. We may not have the technical expertise but we could be responsible for getting it and for responding to the local community in Georgia.

The statewide nonprofit groups are filling a gap that has developed between the numerous local groups and the national organizations. With the increased number of local groups, state organizations can play a vital role in the interplay with the National Trust, the state historic preservation office and the local communities.

A NATIONAL PERSPECTIVE
Truett Latimer

After almost 30 years of steady and sometimes dramatic growth, the National Trust is subjecting itself to a complete physical examination. As with individuals, such examinations sometimes turn up problems that need attention if they are not to become serious. Our diagnosis of what ails the National Trust can be put in better perspective with a look first at some other national organizations.

American Association of Museums

It is appropriate to begin with the American Association of Museums, which is the professional organization for museums in the United States. It also serves individual museum professionals and those who are concerned with the field, such as trustees of museums. Founded in 1906 and governed by an elected council, its policies are carried out by its director and a professional staff from offices in Washington, D.C.

In 1849 a few private citizens and the state of New York opened the Hasbrouck House in Newburgh, N.Y., the headquarters of George Washington at the time he rejected the proposal of an American crown. This was the first American historic building to be shown to the public on the basis of its association with great events and personages. The historic house in America was born.

In 1859 the Mount Vernon Ladies' Association of the Union opened Washington's Mount Vernon plantation house to the public. Interestingly enough, they did not plan to get into the business of historic preservation. The group of indignant women started out with the purpose of securing the house's future through acquisition by the federal government or the commonwealth of Virginia—both of whom refused.

From then until now there has been a great proliferation of museums located in historic structures. On many oc-

Truett Latimer is executive director, Texas State Historical Commission, Austin, Tex.

casions they have started out, not as museums, but rather as attempts to save historically or architecturally significant structures. For too many years the popular thought was to save a structure and the second thought was to use it adaptively as a museum.

Therefore, numerous museum staffs find themselves in the curious position of caring not only for their collections but also the structures in which they are located, with all the cyclical maintenance problems of historic properties.

With the large number of museums in historic structures throughout the nation, one would think that the AAM would have committed itself long ago to helping meet their special needs and problems. It would have seemed appropriate that the new Historic House Association of America would be sponsored by the AAM and would be one of its active affiliated groups. Not so. The organization was sponsored by the National Trust.

The AAM has a good legislative reporting service for its members, which keeps them informed on historic preservation legislation as well as museum legislation. In addition, the AAM has allowed the formation of an affinity group that is made up primarily of small history museums. The attention the AAM could have given historic preservation simply has not occurred.

American Institute of Architects
A valuable committee of a national, professional organization is the Committee on Historic Resources of the American Institute of Architects. This committee has passed resolutions expressing its views on preservation of Grand Central Terminal, the proposed extension of the west front of the U.S. Capitol and continued support of the Historic American Buildings Survey, administered by the U.S. Department of the Interior. In recent years, this committee has been instrumental in leading the AIA toward supporting not only these issues but also the reauthorization of the Historic Preservation Act of 1966 and the maximum funding of the grants program under this federal legislation.

The AIA has appointed a coordinator in each state to monitor the professional activities relating to preservation and to serve as liaison to the AIA, the National Trust and

111

the state historic preservation offices. In some states, the state preservation coordinator has been instrumental in organizing a statewide committee of architects who are interested in the field of historic preservation.

One of the major concerns identified by the Committee on Historic Resources is the need for continuing education of practicing architects who lack experience in dealing with older and historic buildings. This need could be corrected by a major nationwide effort, not only by the AIA but also through cooperative efforts by the other federal, state and private organizations concerned about historic buildings—an effort aimed at professionals who are called on to use adaptively, rehabilitate or restore buildings.

When Philip Johnson received a gold medal from the AIA in 1978, he was asked, "What are the issues concerning cities from a design standpoint?" Mr. Johnson immediately gave credit to the preservationists in our communities whose voices have brought light to the subject of what is wrong with many of our cities and whose presence, not only in front of the bulldozers but also in front of the city councils, has saved whole parts of cities at the same time it was saving individual structures.

We need to be sure that the gold medal winners, as well as beginning architects, understand the role they can play in our national goal of preservation and conservation. The National Trust could play a vital role in such an effort. In cooperation with the AIA, the National Trust could set up a series of educational seminars and workshops for practicing architects throughout the nation similar to the workshops in architectural preservation that the two organizations cooperated in presenting in recent years. This would be done through schools of architecture and state and local AIA chapters, with the help of state and local preservation organizations.

Practicing architects have expressed concern that they are not properly trained to undertake the work necessary to rehabilitate existing structures. Their training has been more in the area of new construction. Architects are well aware that the energy crisis, as well as the growing desire to return to the cities, is making such expertise necessary for them. The establishment of training programs to meet this need could result in great savings of buildings, materials, energy, time and money for all citizens.

American Association for State and Local History

The American Association for State and Local History has established a strong program to educate both the beginner and the trained historic preservationist. Through seminars and workshops, many of which give intensive, detailed training, it has reached those who wish to work in the field as volunteers and professionals. For those who cannot attend the workshops, it has slide and tape programs for loan.

The AASLH publishes inexpensive manuals, technical leaflets and books on all aspects of historical research, preservation and commemoration. The Texas State Historical Commission has found these to be of such great use that we buy them in quantity to send to heritage groups in need of help throughout the state. AASLH publications help people where they are. Perhaps this is its highest and best endeavor. The AASLH also has taken a leadership role in advisory work on oral history, ethnic history and grantsmanship. Its job placement service has helped many heritage groups find trained personnel and many people in the field to learn of job opportunities. Its awards program has given a national spotlight to many historical programs and accomplishments by individuals, institutions and organizations. The AASLH has met success by helping grass-roots Americans become more knowledgeable in the field of historic preservation. I am convinced that the AASLH gives more for its members' dollar than any other such national organization.

Other Organizations

There are several national preservation-related organizations with which the National Trust should maintain a close working liaison. One of these is the Society of Architectural Historians, which is primarily a professional society for the dissemination of information to professionals who are working and teaching in the field. It has both state and local chapters. The national organization holds an annual meeting with a program that includes various preservation topics. It also sponsors foreign and domestic tours and publishes a newsletter.

The Victorian Society in America maintains its national headquarters in Philadelphia. It also has state chapters and sponsors tours that offer information on all aspects of Victorian life. It has published several fine books and produces a monthly newsletter for members. Its annual meeting also features restoration and preservation topics.

Preservation Action was formed recently to provide a national lobbying effort for historic preservation. I believe this organization came into being because the cautious and conservative legal counsel of the National Trust had serious reservations about the National Trust entering this field. Now the National Trust has decided that it will begin a lobbying effort, even though it has just announced a $25,000 grant to assist Preservation Action in its endeavors. Preservation Action has proven worthy of wholehearted support.

There is every evidence that historic preservation in America has come of age. At least it would seem so from the proliferation of specialized preservation groups. It is curious that they use the platform provided by the National Trust annual meeting to espouse their organizations, yet have no affiliation with the National Trust.

Does this say that the National Trust is not doing what it should be doing, that if it were the proliferation of such organizations would not be occurring? While such groups undoubtedly are beneficial, the cause of historic preservation would best be served if they became affinity groups of the National Trust, much in the manner of the Historic House Association of America.

With the continued increase of national preservation organizations, I see the day when private assistance for the practicing preservationist will be much the same as it is today when one attempts to deal with the maze of agencies within the federal government that assist the preservation effort.

Future Role of the National Trust

I think it is time for the preservation community and the National Trust to examine thoroughly and closely the formation of the multiplicity of organizations that could tend to diffuse the effectiveness of the total preservation movement. There is strength in unity and if these organizations

114

were affinity groups of the National Trust our efforts would be better served. For instance, because of the time and expense, the practicing preservationist already finds it impossible to attend the annual meeting of every preservation organization currently in existence. I believe that National Trust-affiliated groups could meet immediately before or following National Trust annual meetings and, therefore, allow preservationists to receive the best and most current preservation information in one trip rather than a dozen.

Liaison with Other Groups

The National Trust has done and is doing a great job, but its effectiveness can be improved. While some relationship with national organizations has been established, it is my firm belief that liaisons with numerous national institutions need to be firmly established in National Trust programs. Liaisons should be established with organizations such as the Urban Land Institute, U.S. Savings and Loan League, Appraisal Institute, American Bankers Association and Mortgage Bankers Association, as well as with all federal agencies whose programs touch on historic preservation, including the U.S. General Services Administration, the U.S. Departments of Commerce, Interior and Housing and Urban Development and the National Endowments for the Arts and Humanities.

It is time for the National Trust to become sophisticated in its capability to transmit information to preservation organizations throughout the nation. The establishment of an appropriate data bank at the National Trust with terminals at preservation organizations around the nation could make information available instantaneously on almost any subject.

One of the main thrusts of the national government in our field is the Historic Preservation Act of 1966. While the basic authority for the administration of this act rests with the Secretary of the Interior, the work in the field is done by the state historic preservation offices. Therefore, it is necessary for the president of the National Conference of State Historic Preservation Officers and the chairman of the Advisory Council on Historic Preservation to be invited to attend and participate in board meetings of the National Trust.

In addition, we should have a national historic preservation coalition involving the National Trust, the American Association for State and Local History, the American Institute of Architects, the state historic preservation officers, the American Association of Museums, the Victorian Society in America and all other related entities and organizations. It is time for historic preservation groups to begin communicating with each other, and the National Trust is the logical organization to bring such a coalition into existence.

Communications

Belatedly, the National Trust has determined that it will begin publishing an expanded historic preservation magazine, a situation that very closely parallels the lobbying effort of the National Trust mentioned earlier. Not until the publication of *American Preservation* did the National Trust decide to enlarge its magazine. Instead of being in competition with private enterprise, we should underline, publicize and applaud what private enterprise is doing in this area.

The National Trust is a private, nonprofit organization chartered by Congress in 1949 to lead the movement for preservation of our architectural and historical resources. Today [1978] it has more than 140,000 individual members and 3,000 member organizations. It is estimated that 2 million Americans are actively involved in historic preservation. The membership of the National Trust has risen dramatically in recent years, the result perhaps of the large sums allocated for the acquisition of new members. But why are the two million Americans who are actively involved in preservation not members of the National Trust? With a membership of 140,000, one out of every 14 persons actively involved in the movement is a National Trust member. Put another way, when we divide the U.S. population of 218,-400,000 by the membership, we find that one of every 1,560 people is a National Trust member. Are these figures of which to be proud if we, in fact, are leading the movement for preservation of the architectural and historical resources in America?

The National Trust secured mailing lists of *Scientific American*, *National Geographic*, the National Audubon

Society, the Wilderness Society, the National Wildlife Federation and others. Should it not work with the 3,000 National Trust member organizations to secure their membership lists? Their members supposedly make up the 2 million Americans who are actively involved in historic preservation. Perhaps a cooperative membership should be considered, such as has been developed by the Historic Preservation League of Dallas, whereby contributors of more than $50 to that organization also were given membership in the National Trust.

The National Trust has been searching for a more meaningful way for its Board of Advisors to help it. One way might be to assign them the responsibility of discussing with the preservation membership organizations in their states the possibility of a cooperative membership. The National Trust regional offices also could be involved in this endeavor.

Neighborhoods

During 1978 the National Trust initiated a program titled the Neighborhood Conservation Clearinghouse and began the publication of *Conserve Neighborhoods,* a newsletter for more than 1,500 neighborhood organizations. This is one of the finest moves the National Trust has made. In a nation that has shifted from the personal to the impersonal, from responsive to unresponsive government, from a sense of place to a sense of placelessness, it is entirely appropriate to begin working with definable geographic areas with specific individuals and organizations to whom we can be responsive. Historic preservation is a vital part of these communities and it must be encouraged and supported.

One of the fastest growing movements in the United States is that of the neighborhood organization. Many of our urban neighborhoods have been victims of the flight to the suburbs that resulted in a deteriorated economic base for inner-city areas. Now people are returning to these neighborhoods for reasons that range from an appreciation of worthy architectural structures to cutting down on gasoline bills and commuting time. Most of the inner-city areas are in poor condition, and neighborhood organizations spring up as a means of getting the garbage collected and other city services reinstated. But the neighborhood organization can go far beyond that level of activity and, as historic preservationists, we must see that it does.

This is not to say that the trash must not be picked up first, because it must. There also must be adequate police protection, fire stations nearby and good park and school facilities before any of the aesthetics can be taken into consideration. Neighborhood residents quickly learn that they can get a response from the city by working together. Then the trash is picked up and the police come when called and parks and schools are improved.

The National Trust can help the neighborhood organizations by providing them with tax information, architectural guidelines, information on funding sources, methods of volunteer organizational involvement, legislation, such as zoning laws and ordinances and other information that will make it possible to reestablish city neighborhoods in a strong posture.

We have heard much about the quality of life, and this is what the neighborhood organization is trying to achieve. The National Trust has made a good beginning with its Neighborhood Conservation Clearinghouse. In Texas, neighborhood organizations are making great strides, and they need and welcome all the information they can get. The Neighborhood Conservation Clearinghouse is the logical source for such help.

Rolls Royce or Chevy?

Since 1957, when Vance Packard wrote *The Hidden Persuaders*, the American public has been aware of how it decides to buy everything from soap to automobiles. Since 1960, when Theodore H. White wrote *The Making of the President*, the American people have known that presidents are elected in the same way we select laundry soap; the same methods of packaging, advertising and promotion are used.

This type of selling is made possible because of the sophisticated survey techniques that have been developed. If the National Trust authorized such a survey, it might learn that it needs to look a little less sophisticated. The National Trust may give the impression of a Rolls Royce organization when it should be giving the impression of a Ford or Chev-

118

rolet. The National Trust needs to ask its consumers what it is doing right and what it is doing wrong. And the National Trust should ask those who are not its consumers what it is doing wrong. It should ask the real estate agents, builders, developers, financial institutions and members of Congress. The National Trust should know what it has to do to win them over.

Such a survey could be enlightening and lead the Trust into making the right decisions about the future direction of historic preservation in the United States. Let us work together to make the National Trust an even greater organization than it is now. Let us make sure it meets the ever-changing needs of the great and growing preservation constituency in the United States.

DISCUSSION

Summary of comments made by panelists, audience and the commentators

Evolution of Organizations

Local preservation groups often begin their programs with a focus on saving a single building and then gradually broaden their interests into areawide preservation represented by historic districts and neighborhood conservation. The recent growth in statewide, private, nonprofit organizations evidences a need for state umbrella organizations to facilitate better working relationships with public state historic preservation offices. The majority of private nonprofit statewide organizations have indicated a desire to be separate and on their own but they will need National Trust help to do so. Some consideration should be given to an affiliated status with the National Trust rather than formation of chapters. While a need for groups to work together has been identified, it often is not easy for preservationists to spend time working with other groups when they need to put their time into accomplishing their own organization's objectives.

There is a growing need for well-prepared, practical information from both national and state sources for use at the local level, especially to combat industry-supplied data on rehabilitation. A basic objective for all organizations should be good ongoing maintenance of property in their stewardship.

Preservation as a Catalyst

Preservationists' current and future problems are more those of success than failure; thus, they need to be able to respond to a new set of circumstances and a broadening involvement by new groups. The role of preservation organizations as catalysts should be given more emphasis; they need to work toward the objective of spreading involvement in preservation to a greater array of private and public individuals and organizations. Our public education objectives need to be broadened by the use of more sophisticated techniques to reach greater numbers of people. Rather than just promoting the joining of preservation organizations, our public promotional efforts need to promote a cause forcefully.

When we unsuccessfully exhaust the existing channels for working with a reluctant city government, we should be ready to work through the political process. The emerging state organizations need to do more to prod state government in terms of preservation and conservation legislation and policies developed by public regulatory bodies. Among the major objectives at the national level are the establishment of a national preservation bank and the need for surveys of the public's attitudes toward preservation. The recent growth in public funding of private preservation organizations should be viewed against the need for such organizations to speak out uncompromisingly to public agencies. While we are broadening our scope so as to go beyond our past of "a happy few," we also need to keep our historic preservation identity.

National organizations should be ever mindful of the need to maintain a broad geographic representation on their governing boards and advisory committees. The growing body of individuals serving in both salaried and voluntary capacities on private boards of directors and public preservation commissions needs to be strengthened through a continuing education process in order to make them more effective in their roles.

Further consideration may be necessary in defining the interests and relationships between historic preservation and neighborhood conservation to assure cooperation between these two interests.

Preservation and Displacement

The issue of neighborhood displacement is a local one, but national organizations such as the National Trust should take a position; how that position is handled locally is the question. If displacement is a threat in a community, then citizens have to become part of the solution. People have been displaced throughout history because they did not own property. It is necessary, therefore, to compete with speculators in the neighborhood who want to buy up a street and then drive out the current population. Neighborhood preservationists will have to compete with them by offering

121

the owners of the buildings considerably more money than the speculators. That is what will stop displacement.

Preservation's Fundamental Purpose

While many people believe that historic preservation's fundamental purpose is the conservation of history, others do not share that definition. While conservation of history may have been the fundamental purpose in the beginning, preservation today also speaks to matters of aesthetics and taste. Some preservationists are beginning to look at how aesthetic determinations are made, such as the design of new buildings in historic districts.

As preservation moves to broaden its role, as it clearly must, by embracing the neighborhood conservation and the environmental movements, a concern arises that preservation's distinctive perspective and mission may be lost as it merges into a broader-based coalition. However, that implies that to lose a distinctive perspective and mission is to dilute or to change something into something less desirable. To change what we as preservationists are about is to be responsive and is to be successful. The preservation movement is going from a narrower definition of historic preservation to a broad definition embracing quality-of-life issues and recognition that change is not a threat.

Relating Preservation and Conservation

In many states, the natural conservation groups may be older and stronger than preservation groups. Today, a sort of liaison is beginning to take place between the built environment people and the natural conservation people. That should not dilute what preservationists are doing but should increase instances where we can make common cause. For example, there may be a time when state agencies will want a four-lane highway to go through a historic district or through a mountain. In such instances we can join forces to fight the threat.

THE PRESERVATION MESSAGE AND THE PRESS

G. Donald Adams

Looking into the future is difficult, especially in the field of communications, where changes occur every day. What follows are some ideas, likely possibilities perhaps, of what our problems will be in the future as we try to tell the preservation story.

Stories must go beyond the pretty newspaper photo spreads that are calculated to appeal to upper middle class readers with pictures of preserved neighborhoods as "enchanted oases" and must reach people involved with preservation at all levels. It will be vital that the preservation message advance convincing solutions to the problems of displacement, energy conservation and coexistence with urban developers.

Emphasizing the urgency with which we must care for the best of our perishable built environment and the role that preservation has in revitalizing people, neighborhoods, business districts and whole cities will be even more critical than it is today. It will be mandatory to involve those most directly affected by the preservation project in making decisions and shaping the message before it is released to the media.

Such specialized communicators as lobbyists, legislators, travel writers and publishers engaged by the building trades, utilities and other important constituencies must be approached to convey the message over and over again that preservation makes "dollars and sense."

Refining Our Message

If support for preservation is going to maintain its momentum and extend into all socioeconomic strata and geographic regions of the nation, preservationists must present their ideas in a clear, meaningful message.

A proliferation of well-meaning but fragmented preser-

G. Donald Adams is print media services manager, Greenfield Village and the Henry Ford Museum, Dearborn, Mich.

vation groups, each with its own message, has often confused the media and readers. The most important element of the preservation story—How does preservation benefit me?—often is overlooked. How preservation benefits everyone must be the consistent theme running through our stories.

Newspaper and magazine readers do not take the time to sort out complex messages. Often they are not interested in all aspects of issues. They are interested in messages that relate immediately and personally to them. We need to reassure people that preservation will have a positive effect on their lives. We need to tell them how they can get assistance. Our message needs to be useful to readers.

Such issues as displacement and increased rents must be dealt with through two-way personal communication. Conflicts over these subjects are treated as hard news by the media and can have devastating results.

Preservation often is a personal matter involving pride, background and taste. For many who wish to continue living in their neighborhoods, for example, the old buildings can be a symbol of poverty. They may want desperately to demolish tangible reminders of a bleak past and build anew. Communication with those whose homes are affected by preservation begins with listening. This is particularly true of preservation projects in deteriorating neighborhoods with disadvantaged families. Attempts to build support for preservation through communication with residents of such areas must be well thought out and made direct and personal. Otherwise, emotional dissension may be aroused, such as that of an area in Detroit where preservation efforts were being made and one resident was quoted in a newspaper story as saying he would burn his house before he would see it preserved. Emotional dissension of that order probably could have been avoided if the opinions of key residents had been sought by the preservationists prior to being sought by the newspaper reporter.

Changing Attitudes and Behavior

Preservation in the future may be presented to the media as a matter of lifestyle, rather than as an isolated exercise. Such concepts as the following too often are being advanced by the media without the benefit of a preservationist point of view: old is bad; old parts of cities are unsafe; buy new to benefit from advances in technology; parking space is the greatest need for the city; only wealthy people live in restored neighborhoods; preservation is expensive; old buildings are difficult to heat or cool, do not use space well, are expensive to maintain; old commercial buildings project a backward image of their occupants.

The preservation communicator must confront our throw-away society with compelling reasons for reassessing the built environment. We should guide the media into taking a look at how spacious old houses can be used in exciting and efficient ways. Assuming that the movement back to the cities continues in the 1980s, pressure from land-hungry developers to demolish worthwhile old structures will only increase.

In short, our preservation story not only has to clarify the facts, but also has to help change attitudes and behavioral patterns. We might get some ideas on how to change attitudes through our media message by studying such national communications programs as those aimed at reduction of energy consumption and passage of returnable bottle legislation. People might be asked to behave as if everything were not disposable; this might be a major behavioral modification.

In our communication efforts we will need all the help we can get. Perhaps corporations more frequently could feature in their national advertising campaigns and annual reports successful preservation efforts involving use of their products.

Commercial publishers could accelerate publication of technical advice for the do-it-yourself preservationist and books on successful preservation projects. The promotion of these books on television talk shows and in press reviews could further promote preservation.

In the future, publications such as municipal travel and chamber of commerce brochures could more frequently emphasize the positive results of preservation in their cities. Members of organizations such as the Society of American Travel Writers are closely involved in writing about cities as travel attractions. They value the preservation of a community's character and personality.

The strong preservation message of the future should incorporate research findings on subjects such as the effects of the built environment on worker productivity and mental and physical health. These concerns are major media themes today. Preservationists must relate to current issues wherever possible.

The Media and Popular Themes

The future is both bright and threatening to the preservation story. We relate well to many media themes that are likely to continue being popular, such as social harmony, neighborhood pride, self-improvement, self-dependence, beating high construction costs, community enhancement and antiques as investments and expressions of our cultural heritage.

The media like stories with a local angle. All preservation efforts have a local quality about them.

The media always are on the lookout for a good story. Unfortunately, failures are good stories. We should expect that preservation failures or the uncovering of misappropriations in preservation programs will make a strong and lasting impression on the public. As more programs are undertaken more failures can be expected.

The promotion of new shopping centers that will continue to draw life from downtown areas probably will continue the decay of the city's built environment. Yet, media dependence on advertising revenue from new retailers could make it difficult for the press to support preservation projects that drive away business. It will be important that the media understand and are supportive of adaptive rehabilitation of existing worthwhile buildings for effective commercial use.

Using Media to Tell the Story

As guardians of our nation's historic treasures and as transmitters of our cultural heritage to oncoming generations, preservationists are accountable to the American public. When the value of our work is appreciated more by the press, the opportunities for helping fulfill our accountability through placements of major preservation stories will be improved. In the future we must use every available method to secure the understanding and support of the media to build a national conscience for preservation.

Families will continue to seek quality in all aspects of their lives. Appreciation for the craftsmanship of past artisan builders has never been stronger. Parents want their children to be enriched by their cultural heritage. Through the media we can urge parents to get their children involved with preservation programs conducted by schools, historical societies or other agencies. Education and child development are popular media themes that can relate to involvement with our preservation projects.

Interest in preservation is likely to increase in the future. We must be prepared to take full advantage of this interest.

As the nation embarks on its third 100 years, enough American history has accumulated to sustain an appreciation for our heritage as a nation. This is evident in the media's high level of interest in American architecture and decorative arts, subjects that are part of many of our preservation programs.

Many Americans who share our appreciation for the built environment quickly become discouraged and do not know how to translate their feelings into action. Making sources of help known through the commercial media will continue to be a challenge for preservationists in the years ahead.

Perhaps future generations will preserve their built environment in celebration of their maturity and sensitivity as persons, as communities and as a nation.

As we approach our next century, we are challenged to tell the preservation story in new ways to new generations. Perhaps we should tell them that preservation is a celebration that makes "dollars and sense."

TELEVISION AND RADIO MEDIA
Herbert C. Gunther

The 1970 census indicated that nearly 96 percent of all American families had at least one television set, and more recent figures show that a majority have two. Almost every household in the country has a radio, and almost as many have two. It is well known that on the average a person graduating from high school has spent substantially more time in front of a television set than in a classroom. And that same young person will have been exposed to several hundred thousand commercial messages. Television sets are on in most households an average of six hours a day.

As these figures suggest, television and radio are powerful mechanisms that shape our imagination, reinforce social values, tell us what is important and what is trivial, what is right and wrong, what is acceptable and what is not, what is news and what is not. One poll has shown that nearly three quarters of all Americans derive their opinions on public policy issues from television. Newspapers came in a poor second. One has only to look at how political candidates spend their advertising budgets to get a sense of how effective television and radio are.

The point of these facts is that despite the obvious influence of the media, many advocacy organizations, including preservation-oriented ones, overlook their use as a communications tool. The reason for this may be that preservationists, like many others, do not understand one of the basic tenets of our communications system, which is that the airwaves that carry radio and television signals are a public resource and as such the public has a right to use that resource. This right stems from the early chaotic days of radio.

Back in the days when use of radio was being established, almost anyone who could afford the technology (and there were a lot of people who could) went into radio broadcasting: corporations, colleges, etc. The result was anarchy. Those

Herbert C. Gunther is director, Public Media Center, San Francisco, Calif.

who had radio receivers never knew from day to day what or who they would get. Broadcasters used whatever frequencies they felt like using, and many used the same ones, knocking each other off the air. It was so chaotic that Congress was asked to step in and establish rules to govern the use of the airwaves. Congress passed the Communications Act of 1934, which, along with other rules, set up technical standards and divided up the airwaves into what are now the numbers on your radio dials. But Congress still had one problem: Even after all the criteria they established were met, there were still more takers than frequencies. So Congress decided on one additional requirement before awarding a frequency: The holder of a broadcast license would have to serve the public interest, necessity and convenience. That requirement is in every license issued by the Federal Communications Commission, the government agency that is responsible for regulating broadcasters.

This is a significant fact, one that many broadcasters have forgotten and the public generally does not know about. The concept of radio and television as public institutions has been lost in the incredible commercial success they have had. Primary use of radio and television as media for advertising and entertainment is a distortion of the idea that the public owns and controls a scarce resource that ought to be used for the benefit of us all. Much of the work of the Public Media Center involves informing the public that it owns the airwaves and that the law provides numerous opportunities for citizen access and public accountability of broadcaster performance. The Public Media Center is a nonprofit public interest advertising agency that produces media campaigns for nonprofit organizations working on social issues. In the process of our work—mainly placing public service announcements (PSAs) on radio and television—we have become rather expert in the politics and the sociology of communications in the United States.

Preservation and the Media

Whether or not preservation as an issue gains the kind of public support it deserves depends on communicating what preservation is about in terms that people understand and care about. The preservation movement now reaches a lim-

129

ited audience; it does not touch the people who are needed for support in the long run to make it something that works at the community level as well as at the national level. Fortunately, the work of preservationists who want to become media activists is made a little easier because the National Trust develops material for use by local organizations.

How hard should preservationists work to secure air time for public service messages? The best answer is to quantify the value of air time. Many organizations are willing to put substantial energy and effort into getting grants from foundations—a month's work for a $25,000 grant from a small foundation. Getting a public service announcement on the air in a major media market for a four-week period translates easily into the same value. A half-minute of prime local time—usually on a local news program—costs anywhere from $5,000 to $15,000. If securing television and radio time is viewed in terms of the dollar value of advertising, it is easy to make a case for putting energy, skill and sophistication into the effort.

But using radio and television means much more than getting public service announcements on the air. Using television and radio means letting the personnel at broadcast stations know that you and your organization know about your rights of access, how to use media and how to hold them accountable so that they respect and respond to you.

Broadcast regulation is wrapped in myth and ambiguity. Broadcasters themselves often are unsophisticated about the rules that govern them. The reason why is clear enough: Until recently, there was no need for them to know. No one was calling them to task for their programming. No one was challenging their licenses. Broadcasters were so busy counting their money they had no time to think seriously about how they were serving the communities in which they were located. And we were letting them get away with it because we did not know that television and radio stations are different from the local grocery store. Broadcasters do not have the right to do whatever they want. They do not own the number on the television dial where we tune them in. Stations are held accountable by Federal Communications Commission licensing requirements.

130

Serving the Public

Every radio and television station in this country is awarded a license by the FCC to operate for three years in a given geographic area. In order to get that license, the broadcaster has to meet all the technical qualifications set by the FCC. But in addition to those technical requirements, the broadcaster has to show how the public will be served by that licensee's programming. Essentially, the FCC requires that the broadcaster determine the most important problems in the community to be served. Then the broadcaster must plan programming through news, public affairs shows or public service announcements that address each of those problems.

As part of this process the FCC requires that each station conduct what is called a "community ascertainment," which is simply asking community representatives to name the 10 most important problems in their community. Generally, television stations conduct the ascertainment using traditional community leaders—the mayor, police chief, etc. However, because of the growing number of license challenges by concerned citizens groups in recent years, the ascertainment process is opening up to include people who have been ignored in the past. Some broadcasters are talking to a wider range of organizations and individuals to determine community problems.

Another requirement that the FCC places on broadcasters is that their programming be fair or balanced. This is known as the Fairness Doctrine, and it is often misunderstood. Fairness does not require equal time for different points of view. It does require a reasonable balance of programming of differing views. The Fairness Doctrine also has what is called the "affirmative obligation," which means that a station cannot duck Fairness Doctrine responsibilities by refusing to cover an issue.

These requirements are an important part of our democratic system because they prevent a monopoly of the airwaves by one narrow interest or point of view. Preservation organizations can use these rights to be sure that the important issues of preservation are covered in their local media.

How does a local historic preservation group with rela-

131

tively little experience in media go about getting coverage from local broadcasters? Begin by making contact with the public affairs directors of your local radio and television stations. Explain why historic preservation is an important issue in your community and link it to other issues that probably appear in their community ascertainments—jobs, housing, the environment. Offer to participate in ascertainment surveys.

Once you have demonstrated to public affairs directors that you are a legitimate organization with real concerns about important issues, you can begin exploring the various public affairs, free speech messages and other community programming available.

When approaching local broadcast outlets for coverage of preservation issues, it is important to remember your rights. Radio and television stations are not giving you air time because they are "good guys"—they are required to respond to critical concerns and issues. If your local media are not responsive, consider linking up with one of the many media reform organizations around the country or writing a complaint to the FCC. After all, historic preservationists are concerned with saving what is best about our cities. We are concerned with preserving the public's right to balanced programming that is responsive to our communities.

EDUCATION
Alan C. Green

The future of the preservation movement may depend on to whom and with whom we communicate and how well we do it. Two things are of concern. First, we should engage formal education, especially public education, more aggressively and significantly. Second, we should do a better job of communicating with our colleagues at the national, state and local levels. By colleagues I mean other groups, organizations and individuals who may come from other professional or special interest backgrounds but share a concern about the quality of our physical environment.

Engaging the Educational Community

As to engaging education, I would like to propose that those who care about the quality of our physical environment care a lot about the quality of life. We must, therefore, engage the educational community because the new generation must come to know and have a better understanding of the impact of the built environment on their lives. For many of us and for many young people the built environment is a given. It is not considered capable of amelioration but, indeed, it is. Young people need to realize that they can do something to improve the built environment. From knowledge can come action, but we must provide young people with tools to enable them as active citizens to make more intelligent decisions and to see opportunities for change.

The message for education is that preservation, rehabilitation, renewal and reuse are all important tools that can improve the quality of neighborhoods and cities, suburbs and small towns, as well as rural areas.

We are not communicating that message adequately to the educational community and to young people. We should examine the educational system, especially at the local level, to understand how it is structured, how it is influenced and how we might connect with it.

Alan C. Green is president, Educational Facilities Laboratories, New York City.

The kindergarten through 12th-grade programs, primarily in the public sector, involve approximately 42 million young people, plus teachers, administrators and board members. In other words, one out of every four Americans is directly engaged in education, either as student, teacher or administrator.

It is important to note that public elementary and secondary education in America is characterized by diversity and that it is primarily a local enterprise. Education, an activity delegated by the U.S. Constitution to the states, has, in turn, been delegated to 16,000 local school districts. Within those districts are some big and monolithic systems with up to 900,000 students and others so small that they send their students to other districts. Some districts are rich, spending between $2,900 and $3,000 per pupil, while poorer districts may spend $700-800 a year per student. Some of these systems are excellent and some are bad. Complex as it may be, it is at this diverse local level that we should engage the educational enterprise concerning the built environment.

Education is under siege; we are not dealing with the boom times of the 1960s. This is not the period of growth, innovation, miraculous change or the Great Society. We cannot go off to Washington and get big grants to create new curricula and run great experimental programs.

The public is somewhat irascible. We face a fiscal crunch. Local taxpayers are concerned about limited tax bases, particularly at a time of enrollment decline. We pay for some 60 percent of our local costs with local tax funds, primarily the property tax. California's Proposition 13 and other tax initiatives obviously have a direct, immediate bearing on education.

As enrollment declines, opportunities arise. Between 1976 and 1984, enrollment in our secondary schools will decline by about 25 percent. This means we are going to have some surplus schools with opportunities for reuse.

There is also a problem with today's overcrowded curriculum. There is no room for breaking in major new curricula; there is a trend toward the basics—speaking, writing, reading and computation. We have to connect with the curriculum as it now exists and with the teachers now in our schools. Our local schools are increasingly trying to move out and engage the community more extensively. The community school-center concept suggests that, out of the schools, other social services in addition to education are delivered: adult education, day care, senior citizen programs, arts programs, etc.

Education is engaging an expanded clientele. One of our problems in the educational field is that as enrollment declines, the normal base of public support, the parent, also declines. Parents are increasingly a minority in our communities; in many communities, education is trying to expand its clientele and put those who are served by education more and more in the majority.

We must keep in mind that the school has some remarkably close links with the home. There has been a strategy for years that, to achieve social change and introduce new ideas, you reach the family through the child and you reach the child through the school. The ecologists learned this lesson well. My children are far more attuned to environmental issues than I am. I do not smoke at home because of the pressure of my children. Not my peers but my children!

What are some of the principles that might govern our engaging the educational enterprise with our concern for preservation and the quality of the built environment? One is to respect realities of staff and budget. Big money is not going to be available for new teachers and curricula on environmental education, the built environment or preservation.

There are many ways to connect with the curriculum as it now exists and with the teachers who care. It may be through social studies, the sciences, the arts and certainly through mathematics and language arts. We should find where, in our own local communities, there are opportunities.

Our subject matter is broader than preservation. We should deal with the larger physical environment, of which preservation is one aspect and energy, urban planning, transportation and water supply are others.

Another opportunity exists to relate to education the management of the school district's physical resources.

Today's decline in enrollment has resulted in surplus school space and buildings, a situation that provides an opportunity to begin working with the school system in the management of resources as well as with the staff and teachers in reshaping some of that space and buildings for other community purposes.

It is important to use local resources, historical and cultural institutions and professional groups. Take advantage of volunteerism. You are the best advocate and the best local opportunity for working with both educators and youngsters.

Make use of available national resources as well. Curriculum units, project ideas and information resources are available. For example, there is a program sponsored by the American Institute of Architects and supported by the National Endowment for the Arts, state arts councils and local school districts called "Architects-in-Schools" that brings designers, architects and planners into the schools as additional staff to work with the teachers and children in learning about the built environment. Hands-on opportunities—opportunities where children can do things—are attractive concepts as many children learn better through this than through writing and listening. School groups might, for example, replan a playground or sections of a school site, design a student lounge, improve the dull corridors found in most schools or create a model of the ideal classroom.

We must not exclude ourselves from the educational process. We should seek out opportunities for communicating with each other. One means of doing so is that of consortia, bringing together around issues those who otherwise might not communicate with each other, for we tend to be pigeonholed—coming out of architecture, planning or museum backgrounds.

Partners for Livable Places
Communication should be on all levels—national, state and local. At the national level, we are experimenting with an organization called Partners for Livable Places, which has 29 member organizations. We are bound together by the fact that we care about the quality of the environment. One of our goals is to learn about each other, what we are about.

136

We want to communicate with each other and build co-operative programs and opportunities. We also want to communicate more effectively with those outside our own constituencies, primarily to raise awareness of preservation issues.

We are concerned with influencing government—particularly at the federal level. We expect to be a clearinghouse for reports about various cities in the United States and overseas and why they are considered livable places by those who live there and by professional planners who visit them. We are trying to define more carefully the characteristics of livability so that communities can measure, test and evaluate themselves in terms of the quality of life, particularly as influenced by the environment, and what can be done to ameliorate problems.

Partners for Livable Places is a model that might have some appropriateness at the local and regional levels so that we can move out of our sequestered and somewhat isolated positions, gather together at the local level around issues, around general themes.

There should be two propositions for the future in terms of communication: One, let us more aggressively and forcefully engage education because that is really where the future lies; and, two, let us see if we can find some better and more effective ways to communicate with our colleagues.

DISCUSSION
Summary of comments made by panelists, audience and the commentators

Local Organizations and Communications

For many preservation organizations in large urban areas, reaching a wide public through the major media may require a full-time staff person. Competition for media attention is keen, with many special-interest organizations issuing a plethora of press releases. The preservation provisions in the Tax Reform Act of 1976 are gaining the attention of new publics such as investment counselors and developers, creating a new communications challenge to see that the contributions of these new participants represent a quality product. An overriding communication need is to help change the basic habits of a disposable, throwaway society into those of reuse and conservation. Many of the accepted public messages dealing with our environment, such as "new construction starts," need to be balanced by the public quantification of "new rehabilitation and conservation starts."

Communications Emphasis

While it is generally easy to get print media people involved with local preservation boards, it is often difficult to do the same with radio and television people. This is unfortunate because having the preservation message in pictures has great advantages in that it comes across hard and fast. It is much easier and often more effective to communicate ideas using symbols rather than words. Television is best equipped to do this. The term "historic preservation" has a symbolic effect, now unfortunately to the movement's detriment, on what we are ultimately trying to achieve.

It is important that our message reach people who live in the places we are concerned about. The interrelationship of conservation and preservation values has to be communicated much better than it has been. Conservation interests do communicate more easily and gain a more popular understanding with their use of symbols, especially threatened environments.

Communications Techniques

Large preservation conferences are beginning to outgrow their ability to serve all needs. Further consideration should be given to differing types of national, regional and state conferences, specifically, differentiating between those intended for volunteers and those for professionals.

The "Architects-in-Schools" program sponsored by the American Institute of Architects could be considered a resource for incorporating preservationists at the local level; it has the advantage of engaging faculty and students in actual projects.

A concern of preservationists should be the better preparation of print, radio and television news reporters concerning emerging issues and emerging fields. One way to do this might be through fellowship programs that enable reporters to take a three-month sabbatical to go into the field and investigate, in depth, particular areas of preservation about which they are concerned. They will want to share their research with others, and their writing will be more informed on the issues they have explored. If such a program could be launched in the areas of livability, preservation, built environment, etc., there would soon be a cadre of press reporters, TV commentators and radio commentators with a real understanding of the issues.

STANDARDS
James Marston Fitch

We face organizational problems in the field of historic preservation, problems born of success. The fact that they arise
is a direct result of the fantastic growth, development and
maturity of the field.

The term "historic preservation" is functionally obsolete.
It describes a state of our activities that would have been
more accurate 25 years ago when preservationists were engaged in heroic battles to save isolated artifacts on the landscape. In the period since, there has been a qualitative change
in our attitude toward preservation, and we have begun to
realize that what we are engaged in is a curatorial battle to
save the built world. The fact that the term "historic preservation" is so embedded in our practice, so institutionalized in the names of such organizations as the National
Trust, the names of all the acts that have been passed and
the educational programs begun, guarantees that we are
going to continue to be called historic preservationists, even
though the term is no longer adequate.

While in the United States this field is called "historic
preservation," in most parts of the world it is described in
more general terms. In European countries, legislation and
institutions are generally described as being concerned with
the protection of the artistic and historic patrimony. The
term "patrimony" is the key word and a useful one, because
it encompasses exactly this concept of the whole built world
being our responsibility.

There is another interesting difference between European
and American preservation concepts. First, the issue is much
older in Europe than it is here. The French, for example,
established the Service des Monuments Historiques in 1831,
and it has become a large, powerful, well-funded and well-
defined national institution with almost complete control

James Marston Fitch is professor of architecture emeritus, Graduate School of
Architecture and Planning, Columbia University, and director of historic restoration, Byer, Blinder, Belle, New York City.

of all the listed properties in the French Republic. In its 148-year history, the Service des Monuments Historiques has developed a momentum and a corpus of expertise that we are inclined to envy. In all European countries and in most countries around the world, the French precedent has been followed, namely, a strong central, national ministry that has control, not merely of isolated artifacts, but of the whole field of museums. Such systems have many obvious advantages.

Bureaucracy vs. Citizen Activism

Perhaps because of these strong, well-funded, powerful bureaucracies, one does not see in any European country the spontaneous, ad hoc popular organizations that have developed in the United States. This is extremely significant. If compelled to make a choice between the kind of activity represented by the bureaucratic action of the Monuments Historiques and that represented by the hundreds, if not thousands, of groups of embattled citizens throughout the country, I would choose the American system because of its growing sophistication and political power. Its main component of citizen activists is the movement's principal strength and its greatest promise.

In the original meaning of the term, an amateur was not at all a hack worker; amateurs were, rather, people who did their jobs for love, not for money. That certainly describes the great mass of people in America who are engaged in preservation today. And "battle" is the proper word. It is not accidental that many preservation words derive from the field of military experience because, in effect, what people in the preservation movement are doing is defending their habitats. These habitats are under ferocious assault by all kinds of agencies. Often citizens and amateurs have only their own strength to defend them. One of the paradoxes of heroic preservation battles such as those fought in Charleston, Savannah, Providence, New Orleans and Santa Fe has been that the battles were locally generated by a handful of neurotic people. You have to be neurotic to be a successful preservationist! Nobody who is "normal" would donate the kind of time and energy required to stop the bulldozers. In these local skirmishes preservationists may not be aided by professional architects, professional land-scape architects, professional planners and urbanists. Instead, they often find themselves battling the professionals because they are advocates of the policies of the local bureaucracies—policies that preservationists often perceive as incorrect.

From Adversaries to Advocates

I hope that this situation will change with the growing number of professionally trained, responsible preservationists. I hope, too, that in this newer generation the line between the amateur and the professional, instead of being a Chinese wall that separates, will become a connection between the two sides that will prevent misunderstandings from developing into hostilities.

Those of you who are amateurs should know what remarkably fine people are being attracted to academic programs in historic preservation. They are the cream of the crop, the best young people in the United States. And whether initially trained as architects, archeologists, art historians, chemists or whatever, that which distinguishes them as professional preservationists is their passionate interest in the built world and the people who live in it. They do not aspire to be creators of new shopping centers and urban sprawl. Their ambition is to work with those popular forces that have already started the preservation battles in an advocacy—not an adversary—position.

It is not surprising—now that the field has become so large and active and, as a consequence, so ambiguous—that concern has developed over practice. In this connection, I sometimes think the National Trust does not fully recognize the critical importance of the partnership of amateur and professional. The National Trust seems often to take the position of spokesman for the amateur and seems to have a certain distrust of this rising group of young professionals. To suggest that there is an adversary position here is a mistaken apprehension and one that must be clarified in the future.

It is not accidental that two new organizations have just now come into being—the National Council for Preservation Education and the American Institute of Historic Preservationists. These two organizations represent the spontaneous expression of two sectors of this new field of professional expertise. The council, for example, will represent those colleges and universities that have course offerings in the field of historic preservation. According to a National Trust survey, approximately 80 colleges and universities in this country offer different levels of special training in this subject. The aim of the council is to bring preservationist educators together to formulate and clarify our objectives, not only internally—what types of students should be accepted and what programs should be offered—but also externally in our relationships with the field as a whole. Such an organization is badly needed because until now there has not been a structure to explain and defend our interests in the universities and in the world at large.

The newly formed American Institute of Historic Preservationists complements the council. The institute will not be competitive in any sense with existing organizations such as the Association for Preservation Technology or the Society of Architectural Historians but will aim specifically at formulating the standards, practices and accreditation criteria for the professionally trained preservationist. This again is an essential development, long overdue.

The mere fact of the formation of these two organizations is an index of the growing maturity of the field. They should be regarded as the allies, not the enemies, of the amateurs. Their primary function is to speak with volunteers, non-professionals and the public, not against them. Then, for a change, this group will find professionals on its side of the firing line—bureaucrats who will sympathize with, be trained to listen to and work with the amateurs.

These developments reflect the success of the field. But both sides—i.e., laypeople and professionals—badly need each other because the battle is far from won. Indeed, in many cities where initial preservation battles have been successful, it begins to seem as if success is sometimes as dangerous as failure. Take, for example, the fight 40 years ago to save New Orleans's Vieux Carré. That success generated a whole new set of forces, including a large tourist industry, which are now exerting new pressures on the historic core. This means that the preservation battle has been escalated to a new level of intensity. In this battle, the amateurs, the citizens who won the earlier struggles, will need professional assistance of the highest order. But the professionals must understand that the battle cannot be won without the amateur allies. This is what these two new organizations will offer in support of the National Trust and its civilian constituency.

PRACTICES
Charles Hall Page

Who are the preservation practitioners and what do they practice? This question reveals something fundamental about preservation. While preservationists share a common interest, they come from many different backgrounds and frequently pursue conflicting goals. Consider the role of the professional historian, sometimes differentiated in the subspecialties of art or architecture, who is frequently cited as an authority on preservation matters even though his or her background may be in medieval or Renaissance European crenellated torture chambers. This may be approaching the absurd, but there was a case in which a "preservation authority" rendered an expert opinion that one of San Francisco's major downtown buildings, listed in the National Register of Historic Places and recently demolished, was not a good building and was not worthy of retention.

Professional Standards

It is always difficult for a professional to speak of the work of fellow practitioners, perhaps because it is painful to acknowledge their existence and, sometimes, success. Nevertheless, it is important to recognize that, as the preservation movement grows, we are faced with more and more people practicing in the field who appear, in many cases, less than fully qualified. In the design professions, those who have given us instant plastic mansard eyebrows on once respectable buildings seem qualified mainly to conjure up gas lamps and boardwalks and Marshall Dillon-style false fronts. Unsuspecting city councils are naive in accepting such proposals, and the results are disastrous. Not only must we consider some accreditation procedure for professionals but we also must continue to develop standards against which

Charles Hall Page is president, Charles Hall Page Associates, San Francisco, Calif., an architectural and urban planning firm, and a trustee and member of the executive committee of the National Trust. He is also founder and chairman of the Foundation for San Francisco's Architectural Heritage and secretary of Preservation Action.

work and proposals can be evaluated. The Secretary of the Interior's "Standards for Rehabilitation," developed in conjunction with the Tax Reform Act of 1976, are an excellent basis from which to work and work we must.

It is essential that evaluation standards be clearly articulated and widely promulgated, but not limited to the authentic restoration the purists might prefer. Designers and architects who profess to be experts in the preservation of old structures, without conducting any meaningful research on what may be appropriate to the structure, still specify sandblasting of exterior brick walls or installation of "antiqued" brick veneers or polychromatic paint schemes for once staid Victorian facades that would put the Barnum and Bailey Circus wagons to shame. These same architects are frequently looked to as preservation experts. Regrettably, they are often the purveyors of instant nostalgia in the design and execution of such projects as Old Towns, malignancies that are sweeping across the country and with which many of our cities are now afflicted at great, and too frequently, public expense. Part of the Old Town trap, of course, aside from the dubious designs employed and the periodization of structures that never aspired to such pretenses, is that Old Townism is a convenient container for a token preservation effort, while open season is declared on the balance of the city's historic and significant architecture. If one looks at cities that have Old Towns in their midst, one frequently sees the essence of a theme park for the tourist. At the same time, that city, more often than not, when confronted with a preservation choice in the other 95 percent of its land area, righteously bespeaks its "already considerable" efforts in Old Town, as if that were enough. It is not; it is a sham that smacks of the tokenism that renders the isolated historic house museum such a pathetic gesture toward the conservation of our civilization's urban and cultural resources.

Where Is Preservation Today?

In addition to considering who we are as practitioners, a second question worthy of consideration is where we are in preservation today. We must differentiate between the preservation of history and the preservation of the built

146

environment. The preservation of history is essentially a recordation process. It is highly valuable to have such a record for the future but so is it highly tragic to acknowledge that in all probability under the current system that record will be all that we have left.

The generation moving through the planning professions today has become dependent on the enormous research and documentation requirements of the National Environmental Policy Act of 1969 and its state and local equivalents. These people produce vast quantities of paper without ever having to deal with the real world in resolving conflicts or implementing programs. The preservation field has many of these people who provide excellent documentation of historic resources but are helpless in formulating an implementation program a city council can accept. For these people research has become an end in itself. Regrettably, much of the survey activity with respect to historical and cultural resources in this country has followed the same course. The product is, at best, limited to a handsomely illustrated volume unconnected to any program for protecting the very resources identified in the survey.

It is perhaps unfair to single out any professional group. Antiquarians as a whole are dissatisfied with the present and terrified with the prospect of the future, and no doubt there is some of that in all of us. Indeed, are we not all practitioners of preservation in one way or another? The waters become increasingly muddy when one considers that historical societies, landmarks boards and other preservation organizations are really practitioners, too, not to mention the regulatory bodies and funding sources that are themselves major activity generators and to a great extent policymakers in the preservation arena. For hints at the diversity of the points of view, consider the location of the state historic preservation office within each state government. With this many players, all playing by different sets of rules, or without any rules, it is not surprising to learn that perhaps there is no profession of preservation yet, just as there are no standards yet, and that preservation remains an amorphous assemblage of similarly motivated persons sometimes working at cross-purposes and indulging in professional jealousies, accomplishing their programs in a

147

few showcase communities and relatively little in most of urban America.

If all this sounds unduly critical, it should be understood that it is meant constructively. The field of historic preservation has grown immensely in the past decade, both in numbers and in effectiveness, but, from our point of view, as architects and planners dealing in the private sector in the city building and rebuilding process, we have a long way to go.

Effectiveness of Efforts

As a third question, let us consider the effectiveness of our efforts. Vast sums of money emanate from the federal government, $60 million in 1979 through the U.S. Department of the Interior budget alone. These sums are consumed as they progress down the totem pole. In many instances they are well spent; the services and information provided by many federal sources and some state sources are excellent. But frequently the process of regulation and administration leaves little left over for implementation. The amounts available to benefit eligible projects are so small that they almost dictate a poorly done job, given the regrettable but typical lack of any significant funding at the state or local levels.

Indeed, most of the preservation activity in the public sector, where the money is, is devoted to process rather than products. This may well be unavoidable but it should be recognized as a fact. The National Historic Preservation Act of 1966 and subsequent legislation are primarily regulatory in nature. Translated to the private sector, they are manifested in the preparation of environmental assessments and case reports followed on occasion by measured drawings and photogrammatic recording, as part of a process that in many cases recognizes the loss of the resource as inevitable. We have built a preservation bureaucracy of considerable magnitude both in dispensing limited funding from the top but also in processing National Register forms and section 106 proceedings of the National Historic Preservation Act of 1966 from the bottom. National Register of Historic Places forms, however, are not products, if we equate products with implementation, nor are the reports

148

engendered by federal Procedures for the Protection of Historic and Cultural Properties. Surveys, as mentioned earlier, too often become research for research's sake. State plans, by and large recitals of past programs and wishful thinking, almost always unconnected to state planning, where it exists, are not products. Products, in my opinion are the implementation of preservation policies and programs on the ground, not in book form and, for all the machinery we have created, there are mighty few when measured against the opportunities that exist. There are exceptions, of course. The Design Arts program of the National Endowment for the Arts has been the most effective preservation generator in many cities. The U.S. Department of Commerce Economic Development Administration grants for public works projects involving historic preservation have been swift and effective. The Urban Development Action Grant funds of the U.S. Department of Housing and Urban Development, for reasons difficult to comprehend, continue to support new parking garages, new hotels and new convention centers, but could be channeled toward conservation and recycling.

The private sector has done its own thing, of course, largely in spite of government policies, be they federal, state or local. One does not have to think back too far to recall the urban renewal mentality of a decade ago, which resulted in urban removal. But most of what has been accomplished in the private sector has been residential in scope while commercial and institutional structures, the focal points of our society, have been lost or continue to be ignored. It may be productive to consider just what the motivations are that bring the Rouse Company into the Quincy Market in Boston or others into similar projects. There is a projected economic return, to be sure, but what are the prerequisite planning postures, the political climate, the corporate stewardship, the personal vision required to reinvest in functionally obsolete structures? We should learn the answers to these questions and put that knowledge to work.

If effectiveness is to be measured honestly, then we must be cold-blooded about it. The euphoria created by greeting preservation comrades at National Trust meetings and other gatherings is a welcome relief from the loneliness and de-

149

spair of the trenches. But it must be recognized that conservation of the best of the built environment is not going to be accomplished by historical societies and landmarks boards. Nor is preservation going to be truly effective in our society if preservationists' energies continue to be dissipated by historic plaques and marker programs, Old Towns and ad hoc citizen committees threatening last-minute litigation.

Enter the Real World

Preservation must become less the concern of the historians and architects and more the concern of city hall and real estate agents. Just as cities are not planned by city planners but by developers, so practitioners of preservation must learn the basics of urban dynamics as seen through the eyes of the public works department, always the strongest element in city hall. More and more developers are becoming converted to preservation projects, partly because of the provisions of the Tax Reform Act of 1976 (although, as written, the tax provisions really affect and constrain only the speculative developer and in many cases provide too much shelter, under the 60-month write-off, for the average investor). But frequently these developers look outside the preservation community for advice on preservation projects, citing inflexible, unrealistic and in some ways naive attitudes on the part of preservation practitioners more concerned with creating museums to the past.

Professionals in the field have to become more conversant with the real world, its regulatory bodies and citizens groups to create a process at the local level whereby preservation concerns are among those assessed routinely by planning staffs and planning commissions and not merely on appeal by a special interest group with dubious credibility. Much of the preservation practice today is concerned less with the conservation and rehabilitation of buildings than with the completion of survey cards, nomination forms, environmental assessments and case reports, all of which are located outside the mainstream of the planning process. If we are going to succeed in this last part of the century, it is necessary to stop talking to ourselves and start talking to those in state and local governments who are in a position to inject preservation as a major concern of planning.

Broadened Preservation Concerns

A fourth question is, Where do we go from here? Not long ago I saw a cartoon depicting two "with it" types speculating on what the next fad would be. It should be recognized that preservation is a fad of sorts, although I suspect it is becoming increasingly rooted in common sense. At the risk of offending some, I would suggest that many of the early preservationists were motivated, at least in part, by being different and stylish. Before the suburbs extended two hours distant and the country's rail and water transit systems were killed off by the interstate highway system, the motivation for reclaiming inner-city housing was more a matter of personal choice than functional, cultural or economic well-being. Now, of course, the advantages of being nearer the inner city are fully recognized. Reuse of existing structures has become the appropriate ethic for the balance of the century, not because the real estate business has embraced preservation but because labor costs, material scarcities and energy shortages have combined to influence strongly locational choice. I would suggest, then, that preservation, insofar as it equates with reuse, is not a short-lived fad.

What we choose to preserve, however, may well be subject to the trends of fashion. In the years prior to 1950, preservation, to the extent that it existed, was primarily concerned with resources predating 1870. In the 1960s Queen Victoria's legacy was rediscovered and the undesirability of Victoriana during the first half of this century was forgotten. In this decade the Art Deco and streamline Moderne of the 1920s and 1930s, even extending to the early Miesian designs of the 1950s, are being celebrated. This appreciation of past styles has so accelerated that there is little more we can discover, assuming that some perspective of time, narrowing now to perhaps 20 years, is maintained for purposes of evaluation.

Projecting a vision of the future, a dangerous thing to do, I expect that we shall see a broadening of preservation concerns. Even though we have run through the stylistic gamut, there are many secondary structures of all styles remaining, just as there are many indigenous, generic structures that

151

are virtually without style. The private sector has in many communities gobbled up those older residential neighborhoods possessing charm and character that were not destroyed by misguided, shortsighted, so-called urban renewal. It is seldom necessary to promote the attributes of a Georgian or Victorian house today unless it has fallen into the clutches of local government or lies in the path of a new convention center. We shall probably see renewed interest in establishing a sense of place in some of the more recent suburbs, just as we must focus our energies on our older commercial and financial districts where buildings cannot be "owned" by most of us for personal purposes and are therefore subject to insensitive treatment by unsympathetic real estate managers. Future preservation efforts will, as now, become increasingly concerned with park and civic design and other nonbuilding resources and the much-deferred maintenance of public buildings. And we shall become even more sophisticated in retrofitting older structures to meet today's functions and conserve energy.

Questions to Begin a Process

Meanwhile, there are three areas that immediately come to mind and about which preservationists should be concerned. The first is the question of history. Most city councils, county boards and state legislatures still consider preservation to be the embalmment of history in one isolated structure. Such notions are frequently fueled by the local historical society, which in the middle of a public hearing on a downtown revitalization plan volunteers the opinion that "none of those buildings is really historic" and what really is needed is money to turn the old Jones house into another museum. It must be made clear that we are not preserving history for future researchers in an archive but rather we are preserving the physical manifestations of our culture, the buildings, structures and spaces on the land for the use and enjoyment of future generations.

Second is the subject of communication. The preservation establishment has at its fingertips an amazing amount of useful information that does not reach practitioners of the trade, let alone those outside the movement. We must become better at communicating with each other and with the world, at least to the extent achieved by the defenders of the natural environment.

Third, we must work toward a refinement of preservation programs, beyond the survey and planning procedures now in use, to establish within the states and within communities a process for conflict resolution with respect to cultural resources. Despite the proliferation of National Register of Historic Places nominations, landmarks boards and cultural heritage commissions throughout the country, we continue to be faced with ad hoc, crisis-oriented confrontations between Mr. Mean Developer in one corner and the goody-goody two-shoes Landmark Preservation Society in the other. This is never going to be changed unless and until we cause to be created a recognition, official and otherwise, that resource conservation is a central part of planning, just as air and water quality and land use are so recognized. Perhaps the term "historic preservation" is a misnomer for the broader results we seek today. Would a planning department or city council respond differently to the inclusion of an "urban conservation element" in its general plan? Are there ways in which local government and the state can be brought up to par with federal policies and programs concerning preservation that are now years ahead of them? How do we minimize and then eliminate the animosity on the part of local governments when faced with preservation policies tied to federal funding? These are not easy questions. There are no ready answers. But the asking may begin a process that will give us some answers.

PROFESSIONALISM
William J. Murtagh

In considering the subject of professionalism, I turned to the dictionary. "Profession" is defined as an occupation that properly involves a liberal education or its equivalent and mental rather than manual labor, especially in one of the three so-called learned professions: law, medicine and theology.

"Preserve" has a number of interesting definitions, the first being "to keep from injury or destruction," the second "to keep from decaying," the third "to can for the future" and the fourth "to keep for personal or special use." The question is, Do we do these things in what society terms a "professional" way? A related question is whether there is sufficient specificity to these activities to call them a "profession."

I think not. Let me explain. Preservation is and has been a cause in America. It is indeed an activity. It has been and remains an avocation for many persons. But as the cause and the activity increase, it has become more of a vocation, and the question of whether it is sufficiently clarified and codified to call it a profession seems naturally to arise in the public mind.

Requirements to Practice

What are some of the requirements to practice preservation? First, one must grasp the need for continuity in society and in one's neighborhood for the health and well-being of the human psyche. Second, one needs to have a motivation and the skills or knowledge to carry out this motivation. This knowledge commonly has been thought to be primarily in history or architecture, archeology or architectural history, landscape architecture and, more recently, planning. The current state of the art adds interests such as law, business,

William J. Murtagh is director of the program in historic preservation, Graduate School of Architecture and Planning, Columbia University, New York City. He was keeper of the National Register of Historic Places, U.S. Department of the Interior, at the time these remarks were delivered.

real estate and banking.

Just as with preservationists, I think the environmentalists should be cited as a new group in our society in an awkward teenager posture. Professionalism does not appear to give any new status to their activities because all the activities relate in one way or another to more traditional professions such as sociology, ecology, history and architecture.

However, the expertise that hones an activity to the specialist point seems to professionalize that activity in the lay mind. When such activity passes from volunteer status to compulsory status through salary, the shift from avocation to vocation transpires. And it is at this point that the term "professional" creeps into the public mind.

Because preservation activity demands that specific academic skills be combined with business and management, the specific skills learned in school need to be mastered in their own right first.

The needs of the new frontier, however, need to be served. It is questionable whether university course work can provide the student with the type of vocational training to which specific academic skills need to be applied. The multiple disciplines involved in preservation can be taught in the university in theory only. They remain to be understood and comprehended fully under application.

The architectural historian, for example, learns his or her discipline in the classroom from a stylistic analysis point of view and does not learn how to apply this knowledge to the act of preserving. That can be learned on the job. In the political world, however, with its budgeting, regulation writing and the paper storm of the bureaucracy, the learning-on-the-job theory does not work.

Many professors, never having worked in the "real world," are not equipped to supply students with the needs of that world. The contemplative academic world is basically alien to the activist preservation world. Preservation in academia thus tends to remain a national landmark concept in which one of a kind is picked as a type specimen.

The Demands of Professionalism

As the concept of what constitutes valid preservation ac-

155

tivity broadens into the many direct, indirect and peripheral disciplines, activities and peer groups, so too does the need for good academic, discipline-oriented professionalism. With the growth of the historic district concept in neighborhoods and the broadened charge of the U.S. Secretary of the Interior through the National Historic Preservation Act of 1966 relating to districts, those safe pinnacles of landmark recognition have melted, forcing us to recognize and evaluate the resultant mounds and bumps of our past, the entities of state and local significance in our national heritage, either collectively or singly.

We are, therefore, pressed increasingly to explain and defend our statements on the historical and architectural significance of sites, especially those of local value. Our judgments are increasingly assailed by the legal and political worlds. We are called on to be more sophisticated in the application of our knowledge. The Tax Reform Act of 1976 forces the need for in-depth understanding of the everyday architectural achievements of the past by persons trained in the academic theories of high-style landmark recognition.

It follows, therefore, that it is increasingly important for us to remain in touch with our disciplines because we are being called on for an increasingly sophisticated application of them.

When there are no organizational management mechanisms to serve the preservation resource person, a responsibility essentially alien to the academic mind—juggling the needs of management, budgeting, legislative responsibility and work—must be grasped and dealt with during the continued application of the essential academic discipline, without which the preservation activity cannot survive. We need a willingness to explore our motives and processes as well as their consequences. We do not do that often.

Finally, we need to develop a balanced sense of advocacy and divest ourselves of the rather sacrosanct messianic posture that was part of the less-developed preservation ethic of yesteryear. Too often we are impractical idealists, accepting preservation as an unmixed blessing, self-righteous in our stance and unevaluative as to the sense of responsibility for our position in society.

Preservation and its potential professionalism are the responsibility of each of us attracted by temperament and motivation to become involved in it.

Beyond the basics of a history of the preservation movement, broad philosophical concepts and exposure to preservation literature, training for a career in preservation should include specific academic disciplines and skills. Once much of the public has absorbed the psychological values of cultural resources in our society, historic preservation should not need to be as vocal, obvious and self-conscious a cause as it has been in the past. The combative words will melt out of our vocabulary.

If we can get more contractors and architectural firms to specialize in preservation design as they now do in hospital and residential design and more law firms to specialize in preservation law as they now do in copyright and marine law, or encourage the development of a preservation-oriented component or consciousness in companies now alien to preservation, then we will have reached the point where most of the questions that beset us today in defining preservation and its relation to professionalism will be resolved. A professional preservationist will then be that person who exercises a basic discipline, having been academically trained within the framework of the activity, preservation-related or not, in a chosen field.

DISCUSSION
Summary of comments made by panelists, audience and the commentators

Characteristics

The big question is, Where are preservationists going? We know where we have been and the baggage we have accumulated. The common baggage we need to take with us includes that of cooperation, resources and communication, that of communication being pervasive in any profession. We need to get into our new role, but are we really serious about change and do we really want to change? It is not enough if we are concerned only about the illusion of change; we have to live with the willingness to change. If we do this, preservation will become a legitimate profession.

There is too often a tendency for a practicing professional to undertake a first, small preservation project and then become the expert professional able to take on all subsequent projects. We do not want to be confronted only by a series of specialists but also must recognize the need for generalists.

As a movement we are at a milestone in retaining our individuality as preservationists; are we to be forced into the urban scene with all of its sociological problems? There is room for many organizations in preservation, not just one. The sooner we are honest with one another about this, the better.

Historic preservation is relatively new as an offshoot of environmental preservation. The values we are concerned about are not just "historic." "Ethic" is perhaps as good a term as any to describe what we are striving for. In achieving an understanding of a preservation ethic, there still remains a need to better define what is of value in our total environment.

Preservation Education

There are shortcomings in any academic education; the ideal would be an integrated mix of theory and practice. While such a mix is available in France's preservation program, it is not currently possible in the United States. The American experience in preservation education so far has not been harmful. One cannot state that the graduate school preservation experience is homogenizing after an undergraduate specialization.

The appearance of special professional organizations in preservation is inevitable. However, the question of special professional examinations at this time is premature.

The Professional and the Amateur Preservationist

A professional is one who, in addition to the normal talents and culture of an ordinary citizen, has decided to create a vocation out of an avocation and practice it. The amateur is and will remain a critically important factor in the whole preservation equation. We cannot imagine a situation in which all the local battles can be won by professionals exclusively. In fact, they cannot. The battles will be successful only if the bedrock support comes from local people who are convinced that the only way to get local bureaucracies to listen to them is to organize. Amateurs are often unfairly accused of being just so many people who come lately to the subject, militant uninformed citizens who leap into the fray at the last moment—when they see the bulldozer at the end of the street. That is when they begin to understand what the planning bureaucracies have in store for them. It is not surprising that local support cannot be organized until the wrecking ball can be seen and the enormity of what is being proposed becomes clear. Very often local emergencies like this have been the nucleus of what proved to be citywide preservation programs. Isolated brush fires often turn out to be just the warning. Citizens should not be blamed for practicing pragmatic, ad hoc tactics. The advantage of being an amateur often is that you do not know that something cannot be done and therefore you are successful in doing it. It is surprising how often viable, long-range programs are developed by a handful of militant amateurs fighting a guerilla war.

A professional in preservation has to have a thorough understanding of what, why and for whom, with particular emphasis on how the process works, how conflict resolution works, what the tools are and where to go to find infor-

159

mation. If professionals are to be tested on the depth and ability of their likelihood of succeeding in these areas, they would have to know where to get the specialists who will be required to make something work. There are too many specialties in preservation for any generalist to be able to assume all of them. Rather than creating a new profession, we have to be much more effective in sensitizing the existing, important professions. The question would be how one sensitizes those who are going into the real estate development business, the decision makers on city councils, the chamber of commerce and the downtown association. Preservationists will still rely on architects for architecture, on archeologists for archeology and on economists for economics.

Restoration Contractors

There is a tremendous need for restoration contractors, especially to the extent that they too can function as generalists. Those who practice architecture are always faced with the problem, Who are we going to ask to bid on this job? We need to sensitize the contractors to restoration and we need specialists in the restoration field.

Preservation Law

Lawyers do not have a category for preservation in all the source material they turn to for their research. It is incumbent on the preservation law fraternity to militate in its peer group to get a preservation citation category. We need lawyers better equipped to advise us on the decisions that were made in the past and the case history of those decisions that we can build on for new decisions.

The Future

We are heading for an age of pluralism; there will be more agencies, more state trusts, more state preservation groups. The National Trust, as we all know, is no longer the only private sector preservation organization. There also will be a broader scope in the number of causes that we support.

There is going to be more money, at least from the private sector; what happens as a result of Proposition 13 is problematical. A mentality currently prevalent in the country says, Less government is better government, and what that

160

means is anyone's guess.

A number of states are establishing commissions to look at the traditionally licensed professions, including lawyers, architects and engineers, as well as licensed cosmetologists, embalmers and taxicab drivers. Over the next five or 10 years there may be a steady narrowing of the concept of who should be licensed. We may begin to put to one side the concept of the general welfare as a basis for licensing and to come more directly and immediately back to such traditional rubrics as public health and public safety.

DEVELOPING A PRESERVATION PHILOSOPHY

Chester H. Liebs

This conference has raised many questions in my mind. For example, is historic preservation about to die, as some panelists have contended? Or is a preservation ethic near at hand—that is, in a few years will conservation of the built environment become part of the mainstream, thus eliminating the need to further articulate separate values and advantages? How many preservationists, both professional and volunteer, feel frustrated when hearing the same concepts repeated to the same audience? Is historic preservation losing its lustre and freshness? Are there any new ideas yet to emerge in the field? While preservation seems to have reached an initial plateau, there is much that still needs to be done to transform the movement into an ongoing national ethic.

Preservation as a National Value

Preservation is at a great threshold. After decades of hard work preservationists have captured the nation's imagination and are having an increasing impact on public policy. Not all of this rising interest can be attributed solely to our efforts, however. Economics have played a role by changing the national attitude toward energy. Other causes include a recognition of the need to conserve natural resources, a heightened environmental awareness, a lack of confidence in modern architecture and city planning and the resulting impetus for the recentralization of the American settlement pattern. These factors have coincided with the period of preservation's most rapid growth. In order to capture the public's interest, ideas have to be sown at the appropriate moment. Preservation has the public's attention. The task now is to transform this new-found enthusiasm into a national value—a deeply ingrained dynamic system of environmental maintenance. We have taken many initial steps toward accomplishing this end by keeping preservation in

Chester H. Liebs is director, Historic Preservation Program, University of Vermont, Burlington.

the forefront of public attention and through the ongoing development of successful techniques and economic strategies ranging from grants-in-aid to revolving funds and tax incentives. We are also beginning to develop the technical processes for the physical conservation of buildings. This growing area of architectural conservation is beginning effectively to mobilize existing technologies to better conserve older building materials, historic finishes and overall design integrity.

I do not see the development of economic strategies or preservation technology—those areas often touted by preservationists as the key to the future—as an insurmountable challenge in a nation geared to financial management and technological development. If we as a nation are capable of financing large-scale urban renewal, if we are capable of building a $15 pocket calculator, we should be able to conserve America's older neighborhoods and to consolidate deteriorated masonry.

Need for a Well-Defined Philosophy

What I see, then, as the most difficult challenge facing the preservation movement is to transform ourselves mentally from the underdogs we were to the leaders we are. To do this we must articulate a philosophy. Unfortunately, many people find philosophy to be threatening, a waste of time. "Let's get down to the nuts and bolts," they say. "Philosophy is just software to get the grant!"

To illustrate the importance of philosophy, let us look at the material world—a ballpoint pen or a chair, for example. We write with a pen, we sit on a chair. We take these objects for granted. However, at some point in the past much thought went into developing the successful synthesis these objects represent. Succeeding generations have accepted these objects as the satisfactory resolution of a given need and were freed to move on to tackling other problems. Philosophy does the same thing with ideas. Philosophy actually orders ideas and solves knotty ethical problems. It "greases the wheels" of action by producing shared concepts, ones that most people understand and can relate to.

Good attempts have been made at defining preservation

philosophy; one of the best was in a manual prepared in the early 1970s by the Office of Archeology and Historic Preservation, U.S. Department of the Interior, which, in defining various preservation treatments for grant-in-aid projects, provided a succinct philosophy of preservation. But still for many of us in preservation, the "buzzwords" are what we really rally around—not philosophy but jargon. Philosophy provides the underpinnings for systems in society that continue for hundreds of years. Buzzwords, unless put in tow of a working philosophy, only spur on trends; with their vague, one-size-fits-all nature, buzzwords are easily misinterpreted.

A well-delineated philosophy is also essential for those whom preservationists are trying to influence. Currently many public decision makers seem to have trouble with preservation because they cannot assess its worth as a competing public interest, and they must operate by meting out their political energies among such interests. A coherent philosophy would help others to assess preservation's relative importance as a competing public interest. Many concerns besides preservation have to be addressed in the nation. We must put preservation into its proper perspective.

As "boosters" for the past 10 years, we have come to believe in certain concepts. Now that we have gained confidence we have to begin both to expose our field to outside scrutiny and to distinguish between those concepts developed during the preservation booster phase that really work and those that are residual mythology. For example, we preservationists use our words carelessly—to the extent that an environmental impact statement would be in order for some of the concepts we profess! By way of illustration, take that tried and true preservation adage, "old is better than new." That adage might serve as an initial slogan to be repeated again and again by the businessman or planner who is just discovering, for example, that Main Street has economic and cultural value undreamt of in the mall and the cornfield. The trouble is that the preservation community is often afraid to shatter a conceptual carrot that leads people to preservation, no matter how inconsistent or inaccurate, as long as it works in the short run. The popular tendency toward the blind veneration of the past

164

without the ability to discriminate relative quality and cultural context leads to the assumption that we are incapable of design excellence in our own era. It also leads to the development of a preservation style—thousands of bars stuffed with Victorian fragments—rather than a preservation ethic that is not only tolerant of design excellence and cultural significance from all eras but is encouraging innovation in new design as well.

Another frequently repeated preservation cliché relates to suburbs and cities; it is commonly expressed as, "cities are good, suburbs are bad." It is a statement superficially agreeable with the aims of preservation, but it overlooks the reality of our present total built environment and our national conservation effort. Ultimately we cannot afford to have people carelessly dispose of any of the built environment because it is in our national interest to protect and maintain the tremendous in-place investment that existing buildings, structures, goods and services represent. Moreover, when we preach that "cities are good, suburbs are bad," we commit a social heresy because the low-income person realizing the dream of a single-family home in the suburbs is already being psychologically preconditioned by the middle class, who have just returned to the city, to think of the suburbs as second-rate. The social implications of our jargon should be considered much more carefully.

One of the most common substitutes for a broad-based preservation ethic is instant preservation by formula— scrubbing off the character of a community to give it that nice fresh "preservation look." Preservation is the maintenance, to the greatest extent possible, of the design and cultural energy in our built environment. It is a relative concept and is not anything that can be quantified. It is something that each individual has to begin to understand. When applying preservation treatments ranging from restoration to adaptive use, it must be recognized that each building, each environment, has relative tolerances for use and change. Each time we substitute a prepackaged design formula in lieu of a careful evaluation of a building, street, neighborhood or city and its tolerances based on a working preservation philosophy, we risk compromising the design integrity and often the long-term utility of the very environments we are trying to protect. Formulas are for the beginner because no judgment is required. The more the public understands the relative framework, the less we will need to impose controls based on unyielding conformity.

Need for a Growth Management Policy

Our other major challenge in the next decade will be to develop a comprehensive national policy of growth management. Every time a zoning permit is granted for another tract housing development or shopping center to be built in a remote location far from existing municipal services, the nation is committed to producing an increased amount of energy for the life of the facility. Consequently, once-routine local decisions concerning the location of development now have national and international implications.

Growth management can and does work. For example, a major shopping mall planned for the outskirts of Burlington, Vt., would have caused the rapid deterioration of the city by removing its economic underpinnings. This development has been initially denied under Act 250, Vermont's development regulatory law. This is an important decision because it is fostering a preservation ethic by developing an economic climate conducive to conserving, utilizing and expanding existing facilities. This event must be repeated many times if our planet is to continue as a human habitat.

With federal government resources shrinking, we must learn to adaptively use existing institutions. I believe that all the systems required for preservation to become a national value are in place right now. A major challenge for the next decades, then, is the successful formation of coalitions, not competition, in programs and services. We must make better use of existing organizations and programs, better use of National Trust services, better use of schools and universities—rather than creating new educational systems—better use of existing publishers of magazines, newspapers, etc., instead of attempting to create new information systems. As long as we can develop a sound philosophy we need not fear co-option. The following three papers will help us define the philosophical basis for a preservation ethic in the 1980s.

A LOCAL ORGANIZATION'S VIEW
Louise McAllister Merritt

The last dozen years have been a time of phenomenal growth and success for preservation. Whatever their level of understanding of preservation, most people have heard of us. Beginning with publication of *With Heritage So Rich* (Random House, 1966) and the subsequent passage of the National Historic Preservation Act in the same year, the preservation movement has been transformed from an unusual pastime into an integral part of American life. It has been a time of great challenge, when preservation has had to move out of its traditional bounds and react with increasing sophistication to the demands of the marketplace.

But if there have been challenges in the last 12 years, there will be even more in the next 12. For now that we have finally made our way into the public consciousness, we find that the rules of the game are changing. If the value system of the preservation movement is to survive in the commercial marketplace, preservationists must learn to play by the new rules—the same ones by which the big boys play. To compete, we have to sharpen our skills, refine our philosophies and extend and enlarge our educational efforts.

Unless we can become as skilled as practitioners as we have been as salespeople, we run the risk of seeing our movement taken away from us—its emphasis shifted and its values perverted. The neighborhood activists and the trendy adaptive use architects have only a superficial understanding of the significance of the things we are advocating. But as more and more of them jump on the preservation bandwagon, their sheer numbers threaten to outweigh us.

Influencing in Our Own Way
If it is to survive and remain healthy in the years ahead, the historic preservation movement must advance significantly in two directions. First, it must do a more efficient

Louise McAllister Merritt is director, Historic Albany Foundation, Albany, N.Y.

job of influencing what others do—both through controlling their activities with laws and administrative procedures, and by educating and motivating them. Second, it must become as good at the other fellow's business as he is himself.

In other words, the future will see us doing a more sophisticated job of influencing government policy, sharpening the effectiveness of our nonprofit and educational facilities and doing the job more and more our own way, by becoming the developers, the investors, the neighborhood leaders and the lawmakers ourselves.

The greatest challenge facing us today, the most important new direction, is learning to cope with our past successes in interesting others in preservation. Many of the concepts we advocate have become widely accepted. Now we must make sure that the real guts of the concepts are accepted, too—not just the words. We must learn to integrate ourselves, our goals and approaches into the commercial mainstream without losing the identity and the vitality of our movement. This means that we have to develop new skills and capabilities in a hurry. While in the past it has been a significant achievement to restore one major building or revitalize one historic neighborhood at a time, the pace is quicker now. We must be able to affect the way in which hundreds of buildings are reused and thousands of neighborhoods revitalized. Just because it's become financially advantageous to reuse an old building and politically advisable to advocate neighborhoods, we have no guarantee that the people who are using these words and phrases understand anything really profound. It is up to us to keep after them and to keep up our educational efforts.

New Forces of Destruction

In the hands of those who don't understand the greater consequences of what they are doing, the new resources that are being directed to conservation efforts today could destroy our heritage even more effectively than neglect, disinterest and adverse policies did in the past.

Think for instance of all those urban renewal departments around the country that have apparently had mystical changes of heart and are suddenly involved in neighborhood preservation projects. At first, it looks as though something rather exciting is happening, but all too often it is just the same old cast of characters approaching preservation with exactly the same mindset with which they approached urban renewal 15 years ago.

Albany's Pastures neighborhood, a district listed in the National Register of Historic Places, was selected for neighborhood preservation by the local urban renewal agency with federal approval. The techniques involved in preserving a historic neighborhood are no longer a mystery. How then did the urban renewal agency "preserve" the Pastures? First, it acquired every building and relocated every family and every business. Next, the agency demolished every "insignificant" structure (nearly half the buildings in the district), including every worker's house, every outbuilding and every commercial structure. Then the heat was turned off and the windows boarded up in the surviving buildings. There they sit now in desolation while the agency tries desperately to sign up a single developer who will "do" the Pastures neighborhood.

This example of "neighborhood preservation" is as much an example of neighborhood destruction as any land clearance project ever was. That neighborhood ceased to exist on the day its last resident was trundled off to a distant housing project. The best that can be hoped for now is the survival of a few shells of historic buildings dotted around in a landscape of parking lots and infill housing. The Pastures is a failure of enormous proportions. Unfortunately, the local government does not see it that way. New projects are now on the drawing boards for two other historic neighborhoods.

In the Mansion neighborhood, the city of Albany is applying for neighborhood strategy area money, and in the Arbor Hill neighborhood the county is applying for special discretionary community development funds to start its own revolving fund. The Historic Albany Foundation manages the only revolving fund currently operating in Albany. Yet we received no inquiries from the county before it put its application together as to our experience in operating one. In both cases, the first step was for the government agencies involved to put a freeze on development in the neighborhoods until they get their programs set up. Meantime, houses that were taken for back taxes may not be sold. Furthermore, there will be a drastically reduced level of private restoration going on in those neighborhoods for two or three years while the programs are being reviewed and put together. The promise of big federal dollars in the hands of uninformed government agencies at the local level has stopped the grass-roots preservation effort cold.

Thus, while preservation has been successful, that success has caused problems that were never even thought of 20 years ago. New people have been attracted to the movement and many of them have picked up on our approaches without a good basic understanding of the underlying concepts. So what must be done next? Now that this second level has been reached, what are the new directions to be pursued? It would appear that we have no choice but to roll up our sleeves and work even harder than we did on the first level. But this time, we must stop merely promoting and proselytizing and start providing hard answers. The preservation movement needs to move in two directions at once. We must expand our coverage to others than just "converts" and at the same time refine our emphasis. Better education on all levels is one of the first concerns; we must reach out to schoolchildren and imbue them with the preservation spirit, reach the workman on the job and help him find again the pride of craftsmanship, sensitize the banker and educate the politician.

At the same time it is important that preservationists rephrase what they have to offer. The preservation movement cannot forever expand its interests without increasing the basic body of skills with which it handles those interests. The science of conserving historic building materials for example, is inexact. It must be a major priority to expand our knowledge in this area. In fact, in all areas of preservation we need to expand our technical expertise and do a better job of disseminating that information.

Defining Preservation Interests

Then, too, attention should be given to the message we are transmitting because it is often confusing to those not having the preservation viewpoint. We need to reevaluate and define our interests. What are we trying to preserve—the "historic," the "significant" or just the "old?" Are we trying to preserve structures and neighborhoods and landscapes and cultural artifacts and historic houses and industrial relics and historic ships? Or is there a difference in degree of involvement, an order of priority? Must the preservation ethic be all-pervasive or do we run the risk of watering it down past recognition?

We know that preservation reaches out and touches every aspect of life, but that's a hard concept to sell. A well-defined and understandable agenda is needed around which we can build a united front. And some of the inconsistencies need to be weeded out before they are thrown back and used against us. We say, for example, that preservation is for all and yet in many instances we apprear to be all white and middle class; or we call ourselves "historic preservationists" and then find ourselves fighting for every old building. This, say the critics, is standing in the way of progress. Why, they wonder, don't we just stick with our historic districts?

Historic preservation in the United States may spring from commemorative, patriotic and aesthetic motivations, but it has long since moved far beyond to deal with basic concerns—housing, economic vitality, quality of life. With slightly different emphasis, these are the same issues that are of concern to tenants' advocates, chambers of commerce and labor unions. They are the issues debated in Congress, state legislatures and city halls.

Why, then, if our concerns are the same, do preservationists have such a hard time talking to others and being understood? Perhaps the answer can be found in examining just what historic preservation is. I like to think of it as an approach or a state of mind, not as an issue in itself. The issue might be the provision of better housing, or the revitalization of a deteriorated downtown. These issues could be approached either from the preservation point of view or from some other. The trouble is you either have the preservation state of mind or you do not.

To judge by the media, a great number of people must have the preservation state of mind because it is almost impossible to pick up a newspaper or magazine or to turn on a television newscast without finding something that is related to historic preservation. But such notice does not necessarily denote understanding. Rising prices have taken new construction further and further out of reach, and the inevitable backlash to 20 years of a misguided public policy of encouraging suburban growth has created a yearning for a return to the cities. This process, which even six or eight years ago had begun to make use of older buildings and neighborhoods as more attractive alternatives, has been aided by the Tax Reform Act of 1976, which has tightened up many of the traditional incentives for investment while opening tantalizing new possibilities for investment in historic structures.

In short, commercial interests suddenly have become interested in preservation projects. A year ago the Hinckel Brewery complex was donated to Historic Albany. The property had been on the market for nearly two years, first listed at $200,000 and gradually lowered to $20,000. An offer never was made on the property and finally, in desperation, the owner gave it away. That was before the Tax Reform Act of 1976 was operational. To date, Historic Albany has had nearly 100 inquiries on the building. Many are from large, nationally known development firms; one was from a Saudi Arabian firm.

There is no guarantee, however, that because a developer is involved in reuse he or she knows or cares about the underlying issues. To the developer, conversion of a National Register-listed mill building to senior citizen housing may be nothing more than a good way to turn a profit in today's market. The structure that to the preservationists is imbued with a special historical or architectural significance may be to a developer no more significant than the reclaimed landfill that was available for development the year before. It is necessary to make sure that controls are in place—such as the certification provisions in the Tax Reform Act—for any law in the future that will provide development incentives.

The preservation movement does have resources and a well-established support system. Preservation is now well established as a governmental policy, at least on the federal level. Existing programs are functioning fairly smoothly

172

and, through the Heritage Conservation and Recreation Service policy planning process and the congressional oversight procedures, considerable thought is being given to new directions. In fact, preservationists have an advantage in this era of shrinking funds because we do not have to get used to losing huge federal subsidies. The preservation movement is used to producing without much money and doing it in a cost-effective manner.

Preservation as governmental policy is less well established at state and local levels but that too is changing. For example, the New York state legislature is considering a statewide comprehensive bill that would provide on a state level most of the programs in preservation now available at the federal level.

Role of the National Trust

As important as the governmental structure for preservation has become in the last dozen years, the real strength of the movement has always been the private sector. And in these challenging times, there is growth and new diversity there too. The growth and increased visibility and effectiveness of the National Trust during the last decade have been phenomenal. Not one of the National Trust services that helped in setting up Historic Albany's effective neighborhood preservation efforts was available 11 years ago. It is these services that make up the heart of National Trust programs today—the advisory services, the seed money grants, the National Preservation Revolving Fund.

Today, the National Trust serves as the dignified flagship of the private preservation movement. With this role has come greater responsibility. With a dramatic increase in members to serve and, in many cases, to educate about preservation, and with expanding programs to administer, it is understandable that there has been some loss of flexibility at the National Trust. But there never has been a scarcity of young turks in the preservation movement ready to start guerilla engagements. Preservation being preservation, some of these young turks are getting on in years but they have all the education, knowledge and experience to mount successful campaigns. Out of guerilla actions of the last few years have come two exciting new national organizations, which, without the added weight of undue respectability, can still travel light. Preservation Action is a national lobbying group; the National Center for Preservation Law is a public interest law firm. Both organizations complement and amplify the programs of the National Trust by concentrating on specific areas of concern. I think it significant that in 1978 the National Trust Board of Trustees decided to make a $25,000 challenge grant to Preservation Action. This decision indicates that the National Trust realizes there is room for everybody within the preservation movement and that once an organization has proven itself and its ability to deliver, the National Trust will step in and be supportive of its efforts.

Much of the structure of today's preservation movement has come down from the top—federal government, the National Trust and national organizations—but preservation always has advanced from the bottom up. Many of the most exciting preservation advances have percolated from the grass roots. Preservationists on the local level are becoming increasingly sophisticated. Ten years ago when the National Trust annual meeting was held in Savannah, we marvelled at how Lee Adler and Historic Savannah had carried preservation into the real world and put the real estate market to work to preserve a distinct historic area through a marvelous new tool called a "revolving fund."

Today the revolving fund approach seems so simple, and Savannah is again blazing new trails, turning a somewhat surprised U.S. Department of Housing and Urban Development into a major preservation funding agency. Savannah Landmark Rehabilitation Project, Inc., has taken every HUD program available, plus a little private money, some from the National Endowment for the Arts and infusions from the Ford Foundation and the National Trust, and combined it all with a dash of chutzpah and a quick trip or two to the White House to preserve not a building or a block but a whole chunk of the city, complete with the poor people who are already living there. And to preserve it not in the frightful vocabulary of low-income housing but with the same preservation standards that were used in preserving Savannah's historic district for the richer folks. Lee Adler is again showing us with Savannah Landmark that we can

174

do it right ourselves.

Doing the Job Yourself

Learning to do it right yourself is one of the new directions that preservationists will be taking in years to come. They will take as their models what has been done in Savannah or in Pittsburgh, where Arthur Ziegler and the Pittsburgh History and Landmarks Foundation became the developer for their own Station Square project, or in New York City, where Jan Anderson and the Municipal Art Society took over the training of craftspersons when the work that was being done in the city did not meet their standards.

The preservation movement must change radically in the years ahead, becoming both more sophisticated and more exact. It will learn to compete more effectively—but as it changes it must keep in touch with the roots from which it has grown. Even if our movement is no longer primarily commemorative, patriotic and aesthetic, it was once. That is the door through which we entered and that is what makes us unique—with underlying motivations different from the commercial developer or from the social activist. Let us remember that and, as we move out in bold new directions, preserve our roots with the fertile ground that for so long has given us sustenance.

ARCHITECTURE AND PRESERVATION
Paul Goldberger

Not long ago I began a lecture with a pair of slides—a view of Mies van der Rohe's 860-880 Lake Shore Drive apartments in Chicago on one side of the screen and a view of Philip Johnson and John Burgee's 1001 Fifth Avenue in New York City on the other side. Mies's buildings are glass boxes—sleek, refined, handsome; they would appear to anyone, layperson and architect alike, to be the epitome of "modernism." The Johnson/Burgee building, on the other hand, has a limestone front, a heavily rusticated base, classical ornamental moldings running across its facade and something approximating a two-dimensional mansard roof—a sort of billboard mansard—on top. Common sense would tell anyone that it is the older building of the two.

The fact of the matter is, however, that the Johnson/Burgee building is nearing completion, while the Mies buildings, absolute classics, are 27 years old. The comparison is a striking one, for it gets to the essence of a curious fact about the architecture of our time: Suddenly, to be modern is to be old-fashioned and to be old-fashioned is to be modern. Our ideas of what is conservative have changed dramatically. "Modern" architecture, the style of glass and steel and concrete that has defined so much of our landscape, seems less and less convincing as the style of the age. It looks old-fashioned to us today. On the other hand, what looked old-fashioned a few years ago—architectural details like Johnson/Burgee's limestone moldings—now seem quite daring, almost avant-garde. The architectural world has turned upside down.

This is not to say that everyone is going to be doing limestone-fronted, classically inspired buildings. We shall continue to see a great many buildings that could be classified as "modern" more than as anything else. My point, however, is that the advance guard of architecture, the high-design architects whose ideas set styles, begin trends and

Paul Goldberger is architecture critic, *The New York Times.*

cause controversies, has begun to look away from modernism. We may see a lot of modern buildings in coming years but they will have a different role from those we have seen before. They will be the conservatives, the holdovers, the buildings that will look to 1980s eyes rather like a Roman temple built as a museum in the 1930s would have looked in that period.

Indeed, a perfect example is I.M. Pei's new East Building (1978) for the National Gallery of Art in Washington, D.C. A severe building of sharp geometrics, it epitomizes modernism's concern with abstract masses and geometrically defined volumes of space. It is a distinguished structure, brilliantly executed and utterly welcoming—but it is not a structure that offers new ideas or new directions for architecture. That is all right, for in this sense the National Gallery addition is a perfect colleague to the National Gallery's original building, the sprawling Roman temple of 1941 by John Russell Pope. The gallery opted for conservatism in 1937 when Pope's building was commissioned, even though at that time many architects were doing distinguished modern work in the United States as well as in Europe. In retrospect we do not mind, for Pope's conservative vision was carried out with distinction. The Pei building, although it differs from Pope's in that it has great zest, nonetheless bears a similar relationship to our time.

The New Eclecticism
We are moving into a period that some critics have labeled "postmodern"; others have spoken of it as a time of eclecticism or of the absence of dogma. It is that last aspect that I like best. I think we are moving away from a sense, as there was for the modernists, that there is one true way, a gospel, a certainty about what architecture should be. Mies van der Rohe believed that his glass-box style was capable of absolutely universal application. Today two things stand out about the Miesian vocabulary of the glass box: First, it is too cool and lacking in sensual value to satisfy our needs and, second, we do not want any style, let alone that one, to satisfy all of our architectural demands.

The best architecture today incorporates elements from a number of styles. It is eclectic in the sense of that word's

177

derivation, "to select." Johnson and Burgee's apartment house at 1001 Fifth Avenue, Venturi and Rauch's houses and public buildings, houses by architects such as Charles Moore, Robert Stern and Michael Graves, to name just a few, are not directly imitative of the buildings of any historical style. But they incorporate elements of other styles quite freely; they are unbound by the modernists' belief that it is necessary to break off entirely from history and reinvent the wheel with every modern building. Thus, we have such elements as Robert Stern's allusions to baroque villas, Charles Moore's allusions to New England sheds and farmhouses and Mexican houses, etc. Architect Frank Gehry recently completed a law office with an interior partition consisting of a set of columns, highly abstracted, with a triangular pediment above—a gentle, humorous, deliberately ironic allusion to the classic courthouses of old. A few years ago, this would have been unthinkable. Not only did law offices lack any sort of humor or irony, so did their architects.

Modernism has lost its ideological force for a number of reasons, and each of these reasons gives us a key to one aspect of the new architectural style that is beginning to emerge. The modern movement originally made great claims to social concerns; its founders, men such as Walter Gropius, Marcel Breuer and Mies van der Rohe, believed that the new architecture would join technology to social advances and, thus, assure the good life for all. It did not happen that way, of course. As their architecture became more and more successful, more a style of the age, modernism became abstract and distant. All too many modern buildings relate neither to the needs of their users nor to the physical contexts around them. They tend to be abstract objects dropped like sculpture into the cityscape.

Shift in Emphasis

Postmodern architecture, at least at its best, tends to be far less concerned with purism—and the word "purism" is a key. Modernism was concerned with the creation of a pure and perfect object; architecture today shifts its priorities to the making of buildings that relate to their physical context, that fulfill users' needs and that relate to cultural context as well. Thus, the architects tend to add bits and pieces of history to their work; they are taking advantage of the cultural symbols architecture has always contained, whereas modernism's abstraction tended to rule out or deny these symbols. For example, some houses by Robert Venturi of Venturi and Rauch allude through such devices as large gables, shingled sides and generous central staircases to the basic images of "house" we all carry in our minds. Some of the Venturi houses could almost, at first glance, be houses drawn by a preschool child; it is only later, upon study, that we realize they are in fact combinations of historical and cultural elements joined with considerable subtlety. This is in total contrast to the modernist idea of "house"—the squarish boxes of Marcel Breuer and Walter Gropius. Le Corbusier declared with pride that modern technology would liberate the house from the ground and permit it to be raised on *pilotis*, as well as permit us to have flat roofs and to be free forever of the tyranny of the gable. We now realize there is not much tyranny to the gable, and much of what is going on now is part of the process of admitting it and coming to terms with eclecticism on the part of architects. Thus, we can call this new eclectic period a time of common sense, a time in which it is realized that common sense takes us away from the purist, abstract objects and toward a complex architecture that relates to the varied, often contradictory, needs of the city and the human senses.

Architects and Preservationists

This is where preservation comes in, for the preservation movement is not based on the dogma of sentimentality. It is based on common sense, on a realization that much of what we have around us is good and that we are the richer for having it continue to be a part of our lives. The directions in which architecture is now moving are influenced a great deal by the preservation attitude. The preservation movement in the last decade or so has helped reduce our culture's obsession with newness for its own sake, an obsession that, obviously, all too many architects shared. The reasons architects are moving away from modernist dogma are varied and complex and include technological and economic factors and a broad range of cultural factors, but preservation is surely among them.

On the other hand, preservation and contemporary architecture are hardly joined hand in hand. There are differences in attitudes between the two fields and I think it is important to take note of them. The gulf is still far too wide; there are still far too many architects who refuse to take the preservation movement seriously: Both sides have contributed to this gulf. Preservationists are guilty far too often of indiscriminately insisting that old automatically means good. Preservationists also have failed to make proper judgments about rehabilitation, calling for literal restoration in cases where it is hardly necessary or for literal reconstruction to match older neighbors. On the other hand, if preservationists do believe that old must mean good, architects have too often given them sufficient reason to believe the converse—that new must mean bad. That isn't true either and the preservation movement cannot go on acting as if it were so.

A great deal of the force of the preservation movement comes from contemporary architecture's failure to build well, its failure to build in a style that satisfies the needs of our cities and the needs of our senses. A lot of our belief in preservation comes from our fear of what will replace buildings that are not preserved; all too often we fight to save not because what we want to save is so good but because we know that what will replace it will be no better.

Now, at long last, architects are beginning to see the failures of modern architecture and alter their ways. The new eclecticism is an aesthetic that recognizes the lessons of preservation and seeks to integrate them into designs that will be fresh and new, yet humane and respectful of what is around them. We shall continue to see glass boxes but there will not be so many of them and they will have to justify themselves in ways that they have not done before. There also will be an increasing number of literal revivalist buildings—buildings that reproduce historical style, something that was done in the 1920s but which fell into such disfavor in the modern period that it was never done by so-called "serious" architects. Now such things are seen again and we do not laugh as quickly when the French classical addition to the Frick Collection or the mock-Roman villa Getty Museum appear. I still prefer a more creative, interpretive sort of eclecticism but I tend to take such buildings as the ones just mentioned seriously in a way I would not have done a few years ago—another evidence of preservation's impact on our consciousness.

There used to be a lot of talk, when modernism was "hot," of the "spirit of the times." Buildings that were old, or looked like buildings that were old, were considered invalid because they did not match the spirit of the times. Now we know how empty, how shallow, such notions are; they pretend to profundity but in the final analysis mean little. The spirit of the time right now is that there is not a single spirit of the time; there are many. There are no guidelines, no rules, no certainties. It is a hard time to be an architect, for the models are not there as they were in the days when modernism's ideology was unshakable and you knew that you could always win with a glass box. But a time such as the present allows us one real advantage: There is no way of measuring things against an abstract set of rules, so quality can be judged on its own merits. We are freer to evaluate streets, buildings, entire cities, on the basis of what works and what gives pleasure. If the spirit of our time is anything, it is respectful of quality and of common sense. These are basic to preservation and, happily, they are becoming more and more basic to architecture, too.

ON PRESERVING AMERICA: SOME PHILOSOPHICAL OBSERVATIONS
Roderick S. French

Perhaps the most effective expression of Jean-Paul Sartre's relentless vision of the absurdity of human existence is to be found in his philosophical novel with the engaging title, *Nausea*. The central figure of the story is a historian who becomes increasingly alienated from his vocation as a result of insights into the indifference of the universe to human aspirations. He clings to a neurotic survival routine in the relative safety of a city. Near the end of the book he confides:

> I am afraid of cities. But you mustn't leave them. If you go too far you come up against the vegetation belt. Vegetation has crawled for miles towards the cities. It is waiting. Once the city is dead, the vegetation will cover it, will climb over the stones, grip them, search them, make them burst with its long black pincers; it will blind the holes and let its green paws hang over everything. You must stay in the cities as long as they are alive; you must never penetrate alone this great mass of hair waiting at the gates; you must let it undulate and crack all by itself. In the cities, if you know how to take care of yourself, and choose the times when all the beasts are sleeping in their holes and digesting, behind the heaps of organic debris, you rarely come across anything more than minerals, the least frightening of all existants. (Sartre, *Nausea*).

I cite this passage from Sartre not for its implied view of suburbia but because it suggests a philosophical perspective on historic preservation in which the more elite projects and ordinary home maintenance can be seen to have a fundamental affinity. The architecturally elegant, showcase restoration projects and the weekend exertions of Henry Homeowner simply represent different ways of paying one's "dues" to the ongoing enterprise of civilization. Sartre's bleak view seems confirmed by the fatigue and indebtedness of all of us who try to maintain our own residences against the ravages of nature.

The admittedly provocative citation from Sartre was chosen in part to force consideration of the proposition that the

Roderick S. French is director, Division of Experimental Programs, and member of the philosophy faculty, The George Washington University, Washington, D.C.

work of philosophers may have some relevance for those engaged in preserving the built environment. At a time when preservationists are turning more and more to such practical professions as law and economics, it may seem out of step, if not regressive, to ask your attention for the thoughts of an academic humanist. The utility of the humanist is not commonly a first principle in the thinking of modern policymakers.

Of course all of us who make our lives—and our livings—in the humanities remember a time when humanists were prominent and indispensable figures in public life. I have in mind the Italian city-states during the Renaissance. At that time, humanist scholars handled state correspondence, represented their sovereigns on diplomatic missions and wrote orations and poetry to celebrate great civic occasions. But, alas, in the 16th century this class of scholars began a long decline into disgrace and neglect. Their ambition and poor judgment were responsible, in part, but they were also the victims of deep social changes. The rise of the middle class and the democratic revolutions of the 18th century further displaced humanists from positions of influence. And then industrialization and technology placed a premium on a set of new skills. Those who persisted in studying the humanities were forced to the margins of public life. Their places have been taken by new cadres of professionals, people trained in the specialized knowledges of the modern world.

The Danger of Expertise

This brief excursion into history was made in order to arrive at my first point regarding the future of the preservation movement. As I read the literature of the movement, there appears to be a growing desire for "expertise," for uniform standards, measurable data, certified practitioners, etc. This trend is entirely understandable and in some ways to be commended. And as the movement seeks a larger and larger share of public money, the requirement of accountability will become more insistent.

I wish simply to point out a danger in this trend. There is a high price to be paid for professionalization. The preservation movement needs engineers, lawyers, economists and other technicians of contemporary society but not to the exclusion of generalists, those whom we might call the "professional amateurs." Preservation is a humanistic movement, inspired by basic human motives. Its core constituency and leadership must remain people who can speak to one another and to all parties—and not merely in the language of numbers and dollars. In the words of the Charter of Machu Picchu, the 1978 manifesto of architectural and planning principles sponsored by Universidad Nacional Fedenco Villareal in Lima, Peru, "the spirit of tolerance and understanding in human communication is a primary element of urban life." Those who have been trained in the humanities have been educated to have an imaginative understanding of the life experiences of those who live, temporally and culturally, far beyond the bounds of their own life. Nothing is more critical for the preservation of urban civilization than this capacity to understand and respect the meaning of artifacts and historical associations that are valued by members of cultural groups other than one's own.

A recurrent theme in recent preservation discussions is the longing for deliverance by experts, and the related fear that "excessive public involvement" will interfere with the work of "the professionals." I recognize this longing. It is the Dream of Rationality that has animated the prideful achievements and disasters of Western civilization since the Renaissance.

Quite clearly one motivation behind our modern love affair with "expertise" is the desire to escape from the burden of the range of choices required of us. There is a utopian promise implicit in the vision of a world divided into ever-narrower specialties presided over by ever-better-trained experts. This dream of the rational division and management of human affairs is an old one.

The utopian scheme that comes first to the minds of all of us, no doubt, would be that of Plato's ideal Republic, so eloquently sketched and justified in the dialogue of that title. Plato's advocacy was so seductive and so seemingly irrefutable because he proposed that supreme authority be vested in an elite constituted of experts, not in technological fields, but experts in the art of living the good life. Who could wish for a more benevolent governance? But, as you

184

will remember, this rule by the enlightened and virtuous turned out to imply a totalitarian state with every citizen's existence thoroughly regimented.

I suspect, however, that the utopianism that circulates in our blood is not the ethical-religious vision of Plato. It is, rather, that of the father of the modern scientific enterprise, Sir Francis Bacon. Bacon called for a fully subsidized scientific community set apart to perfect the theories and inventions that would enable mankind to recover that life of effortless abundance that, according to the Book of Genesis, we enjoyed in our original condition. At one stroke, Bacon linked the instrument of modern empiricism to the realization of our most ancient longings. In our present troubles we may sometimes forget the glorious optimism with which our modern age began.

The best minds coming out of the Renaissance were convinced that all things were possible, if only we could find the right method. And they believed the method was to be found in the mathematical sciences. Bacon's contemporary and coconstructor of the plan of modernism, Descartes, wrote an ingenuous little manifesto for the new way of doing things, entitled appropriately, *Discourse on Method.* There is the famous passage in which he recounts almost offhandedly how one day he shut himself up in a warm room and invented modern philosophy from scratch. What you may not remember is that the heart of his inspiration was the conclusion that the method of reasoning employed in the mathematical sciences could be applied to all facets of life with comparable results in terms of certainty and efficiency. There is a straight line running from Descartes's overheated meditations and the modern cost-benefit calculus.

In the present context, it is striking to see that in the course of outlining the rules of a rigorous methodology, Descartes, in this most formative of modern documents, takes his first illustration from the field of city planning. His preferences should come as no surprise.

I remained all day alone in a warm room. There I had plenty of leisure to examine my ideas. One of the first that occurred to me was that frequently there is less perfection in a work produced by several persons than in one produced by a single hand. . . . Similarly, those ancient towns which were originally nothing but hamlets, and in the course of time have become great cities, are ordinarily very badly arranged compared to one of the symmetrical metropolitan districts which a city planner has laid out on an open plain according to his own designs . . . when we observe how the streets are crooked and uneven, one would rather suppose that chance and not the decisions of rational men had so arranged them. (Descartes, *Philosophical Essays: Discourse on Method*)

What Bacon and Descartes articulated were not merely the rules for the doing of good science, but what they regarded as the necessary rules for the building of the good society. In their view the model for all fields of endeavor was to be derived from the mathematical sciences. Following their advice has led to the spectacular achievements of the specialized disciplines such as economics, physics, psychology and the rest. But those achievements have been purchased at a heavy price.

It is as if a treaty had been negotiated at the beginning of the modern era whereby each set of specialists agreed not to ask certain questions. Otherwise they could never have gone forward. If, for example, the physicist were to ask the questions that the psychologist asks, he could never get on with the business of physics. The same is true of all the disciplines of knowledge. Their brilliant products require the rigorous exclusion of data regarded by their respective disciplines as irrelevant. The net result is that we are left in a fragmented condition of narrow excellences unable to communicate with one another.

To say this much is merely to open the door on an immense problem. All that can be done at the moment is to point out that the preservation movement has walked right into the midst of these very sophisticated difficulties. The warning from those who arrived at these perplexities somewhat earlier would be that one must always be aware of the number of other decisions one is making when one adopts a methodology. In my view, the study of human problems—and preservation is a profoundly human concern—must always be a multidisciplinary study. I will close this section with an extract from John Dewey's humanistic correction of the legacy of Bacon and Descartes.

There is no kind of inquiry which has a monopoly on the honorable title of knowledge. The engineer, the artist, the historian, the man of

186

affairs attain knowledge in the degree they employ methods that enable them to solve the problems which develop in the subject matter they are concerned with.

In fact, the painter may know colors as well as the physicist; the poet may know stars, rain and clouds as well as the meteorologist; the statesman, educator and dramatist may know human nature as truly as the professional psychologist; the farmer may know soils and plants as truly as the botanist and minerologist. (Dewey, *Quest for Certainty*).

Dewey, of course, was not proposing to weaken our commitment to the rigorous application of scientific method. He was simply working out modifications required for its successful application to human concerns.

Value of the Humanist

Only humanists were left out of that treaty. Humanists ask the questions others do not ask. Or rather, humanists ask as a matter of professional training those questions that others ask only in their private moments. Humanists begin and end with those questions that other disciplines have agreed not to raise. Little questions such as, Why are we doing this? or, What would you like to see happen?

These last, of course, are questions of value. And they are at the heart of the preservation movement. By continuing to be a broadly humanistic movement, preservation can make valuable and wide-ranging contributions to late 20th-century America. But to do so it must democratize its aims.

What kind of broad contributions to American life could be expected from a more democratic preservation movement? For one thing, the preservation debate could help clarify our understanding of the public interest or common good.

We in the United States have an acute need to counter the drift of what is being called the "me generation." The public seems to be fragmented into smaller and smaller units of interest. It is as if we were determined to fulfill an observation made by Alexis de Tocqueville, the French analyst of American life in the 1830s. In his classic study of our civilization, de Tocqueville carefully explained to his European readers that American "individualism" was not the same thing as egoism but was always in danger of sliding into selfishness. It is the opinion of many that we have slid.

This is one reason why the debates in every community

as to what to preserve, and why, should be made more public, not less. All important decision making should not be given over to "experts." Increased expertise should be balanced with broader public participation in procedures and processes. The very exercise can contribute to the search for a persuasive, authoritative notion of public interest. To be effective, the renewed sense of public interest must reflect the population diversity and cultural pluralism of the nation.

A rich, meaningful life for humankind requires a continuity of layers of material and social culture. The preservation movement has made that point most eloquently. But the material basis for that sense of continuity must be preserved for all segments of society in a democracy.

Although the health and success of the preservation movement require the stimulation of more and more debates at the local level, we should beware of the dogmatic localists who admonish us to reduce our efforts at the national level. In the 1980s, the argument regarding the meaning of America may well become more acute, even nastier than it was in the 1960s. If that comes about, any movement truly interested in constructive changes in the organization and quality of public life that does not have strong national institutions, clearly stated national policies and an able and imaginative national leadership will surely lose the argument as to what kind of country we are and wish to become. As just one emphasis of policy, the stress on local initiatives and local constituencies is no doubt politically smart. As an overriding policy, I am convinced that it would prove self-destructive for the preservation movement.

Beyond these judgments as to political strategy, emphasis on localism raises challenging questions of political philosophy. Can there be national policy guidelines for historic preservation that are more than mere generalities or must we allow a patchwork of local standards? Perhaps the most useful national "policy" is one that mandates a process that allows for the continuous modification of standards as the result of an ongoing dialectic of legitimate national, regional and local interets. It is the impossibility of resolving the issue of standards once and for all in a pluralistic, dynamic democracy that makes it mandatory to have a national policy that assures that the dialectic is allowed to have full play.

But we can press even harder on the question of the ultimate authority of local standards. I suppose that if the people of Chicago want to tear down all structures less than 50 stories high, we must, however reluctantly, allow them the right to do so. And if the folks in a certain Vermont town decide that they want a McDonald's on the village green, there are limits to our right to stop them.

In the end, local communities have strong rights, but in the meantime we have the obligation to try to convince them that they might live to regret such an innovation—however much the whole world loves a Big Mac. There must be limits to localism just as there are limits to individualism in American society. At the least, we owe one another the obligation to argue about the appropriateness of our significant public behaviors. Particularly is this true when the scope of local decisions is far broader than local interests perceive them to be. I will mention just two considerations that seem to me to seriously qualify unlimited local prerogative in preservation matters.

The first is what is commonly termed our obligation to future generations. I will have more to say about this later. It is not an easy concept to handle politically, but it is an understandable notion and one that puts some real limits on the rights of the present generation to irreparably modify the human landscape.

The second qualification is perhaps less grand and more readily comprehensible. I have in mind the demographic fact of the almost incessant mobility of Americans in the latter half of the 20th century. I believe that this imposes on us a responsibility to one another to retain important vestiges of local history in order to keep them available for new residents in a neighborhood or new citizens of an urban community. How else will these newcomers find those points of contact with the continuity of human settlement and human endeavor that are critical to the development of personality and the stability of society? Upon adequate reflection, very few local decisions are merely local decisions.

The City and Cultural Diversity

It need not be emphasized that preservation is a delicate task. The one thing preservation must not do is block the normal processes of change by turning dynamic, living cities into static museums. The survival power of cities is correlated with the preservation of cultural diversity. The greater the heterogeneity of an urban community's usable past, the greater the potential richness and strength available to its citizens today. All insightful statements on urban civilization, from Jane Jacobs's *Death and Life of Great American Cities* (Random House, 1961) to the new Charter of Machu Picchu, identify diversity as the key to the vitality and viability of city life.

The suburban movement of the last 100 years provides a lesson on this point. As if orchestrated by a master plan, suburbanization produced carefully differentiated enclaves scattered throughout every metropolitan region. This left society so divided by socioeconomic factors and political jurisdictions that we were morally and politically handicapped in responding to the forces of social change that confronted all cities in the 1960s. Even if we had had the will to act collectively to meet the environmental, interracial and intergenerational challenges of that decade, we lacked the necessary social knowledge and the political instrumentalities to do so.

There is a genuine danger that the current back-to-the-city movement will merely reproduce that error. It could happen that the ideal suburb, as understood a generation ago, and the ideal restored urban neighborhood in 1980 will have two things in common: isolation and sterility. What a hollow victory it will be if preservation succeeds in restoring everything about our cities except their livingness. I assume that it now has been conclusively demonstrated to the satisfaction of even the most die-hard disciple of Adam Smith that, left to itself, the market will not foster this diversity. We must have deliberate and tough public policies if that is our objective.

This constitutes a clear test of the democratic heart of preservation. Learning the values that make a democracy work must come through significant common experiences. Preservation can either reinvigorate our sense of belonging

190

to the same community with shared goals or contribute to further fragmentation into homogenized units.

Preservation and Future Generations

Another broad area of public life in which preservation can make a distinctive contribution is in strengthening our sense of obligation to future generations. This will represent a revolutionary reorientation in American attitudes, but it is one that must come about rapidly. The great achievement of the American experiment in the 18th century was the creation of a civic society whose processes of government were responsive to the needs of "the living generation." Two centuries later the demands of the present generation are of such magnitude and press so relentlessly on the government for unfettered satisfaction as to raise widespread concern that we soon may exhaust the material basis of the American way of life.

We all remember Thomas Jefferson's ringing assertion that the earth belongs to the living. What Mr. Jefferson actually said was that "the earth belongs *in usufruct* to the living." "Usufruct" is not exactly a household word in most settings, but among preservationists it ought to be a sacred term. Holding something in usufruct means using and enjoying the benefits of something that belongs to another— in this case to the human species.

I know that it sounds un-American to some, but I believe that we must generalize the habit of mind required by the National Environmental Policy Act of 1969. We must learn to evaluate the impact of our major initiatives before acting.

Once again de Tocqueville supplies the text that is needed. Writing 150 years ago, de Tocqueville expressed his amazement at this "happy republic" that had the "luxury" of making "reparable mistakes." That luxury has vanished. We must rehabilitate one of the restraints on individual initiative articulated by the father of our doctrine of private property, John Locke. It was, said Locke, an obligation of each appropriator of the stock of the earth to leave "enough and as good" for others.

Given the present economic and environmental conditions, preservation is no longer a matter of taste but a mandatory expression of basic social responsibility. Urban con-

191

servation in particular should be seen not as a private endeavor in behalf of one's heirs but as the maintenance of a legacy for the species.

This relates to another concern on which Thomas Jefferson took the wise position but failed to convince his countrymen. Already in 1784 Jefferson was lamenting the "unhappy prejudice" in the new nation against building houses of brick or stone. He wanted to eradicate this prejudice, he said, otherwise every half century our country would become a tabula rasa on which it would be necessary to build anew. On the other hand, "when buildings are of durable materials, every new edifice is an actual and permanent acquisition to the state, adding to its value as well as to its ornament." The growing sentiment against the notion of throwaway cities would suggest that we have at last matured to Jefferson's perspective. The custodians of the past are in fact guardians of the future.

Transforming Values

The great potential contribution of preservation to American life is not in the saving of structures per se but in the transformation of the values by which we live. The challenging questions confronting the preservation movement are sensibility questions. There is a line from Thoreau that makes the point. On learning that a dam was to be constructed across the Concord River, Thoreau asked: "Who hears the fishes when they cry?" That was not sentimentality. It stemmed from a sincere sensibility.

We can readily develop the variations of Thoreau's question to be addressed to historic preservationists. Who remembers our anonymous ancestors? Who cares for those who will always have to live in housing owned by someone else, assuming they can find and afford any decent shelter? Who feels the terror of future generations who may be born into a world in which the material basis of a good life has long since been exhausted? If the preservation movement grapples with the issues implied by these questions, it need not be uncomfortable in a democracy. A legitimate claim to broader public support requires that it do so.

DISCUSSION
Summary of comments made by panelists, audience and the commentators

Planning

We are entering a period in which we must: (1) develop a clearer public perception of our goals, (2) avail ourselves of the opportunity to select issues to work with, rather than only respond to, (3) assure that our preservation projects are designed for and work with people, and (4) achieve a high standard of quality in our work.

One of the things we learned from the 1960s was to be far more sophisticated about power in our society and to recognize that there are plenty of individuals who know where the power is. They have no bashfulness about manipulating the levers of power, not in the public interest but rather in their private interests. Therefore, the rest of us ought not to have a kind of false moralism about becoming politically involved.

The past 15 years have seen a turnaround in the planning schools with regard to the social aspects of planning. One has to acknowledge the influence of Jane Jacobs and the rapid way in which her concerns have been accepted. The 1978 Charter of Machu Picchu, which is a direct successor to the 1930s Charter of Athens, is evidence that the planning profession leadership is responsive.

Architecture

Many public policies affecting the built environment still evidence by their results a sense of brutalism toward important parts of our cities. While some architects may be moving toward a didactic eclecticism, so far this movement has not had any effect on the way architects are trained to design new buildings in relation to significant existing buildings.

We must be careful not to create a "preservation style"; we must understand and respect diversity in what we preserve. While we should be conscious of the future need to preserve elements of our contemporary environment, we

193

must recognize that attrition in our contemporary building stock will result from changes in economic utility and that preservation choices will be made from among the future survivors.

Economics in the future will be a crucial factor in architecture. A prime factor moving us in this direction is energy. Buildings cannot be built as they used to be. The nation is in a period of evolution toward economically viable designs that will satisfy us in a way that a city of glass buildings cannot.

Neighborhoods

Since the end of World War II, the history of American housing in metropolitan areas has been far from a free-market operation. The various subsidies in housing have demonstrated that what economists love to call "incentives" and "disincentives" have really determined the apparent preferences of so many homeowners.

In order to avoid the prospect of a "Johannesburgization" of major American cities—i.e., the young, wealthy, white professionals in the central city surrounded by suburbanized minorities—changes are needed in our consciousness, our values and the rigors of segregated use zoning.

Individuals

It should be expected that in the future, just as in the past, many of the new preservation ideas will continue to come from the local amateurs, volunteers and contributors to the preservation movement. With a willingness to grow, be flexible and change, they should not consider themselves an "endangered species" within the movement.

PART 4:
ISSUE PAPERS

INTRODUCTION

Following its review of presentations and discussion from the Future Directions Symposia at the Chicago annual meeting, the committee on the National Preservation Conference suggested that National Trust staff prepare a series of brief "issue papers" to be sent in advance to the invited participants of the March 1979 Williamsburg conference. Written from a national perspective on the work of the private sector, they stimulated further thought and discussion at the conference and, it is hoped, will serve the same purpose for readers of *Preservation: Toward an Ethic in the 1980s.*

The National Trust staff participating in the preparation of issue papers included:

Gregory E. Andrews
Aubra Anthony
Cynthia L. Emrick
John L. Frisbee
Frank B. Gilbert
James Harman
William B. Hart
Richard W. Haupt
April M. Hockett
Russell V. Keune
Antoinette J. Lee
Diane R. Maddex
Henry McCartney
Mary C. Means

Terry B. Morton
Brigid Rapp
Michael Richman
Theodore A. Sande
Mary Lou Schleck
Lyn Snoddon
Lois Snyderman
Philip D. Spiess
Samuel N. Stokes
Hisashi Bill Sugaya
Kathryn Welch
Patricia Williams
Dwight L. Young

PRIVATE PHILANTHROPY AND PRESERVATION

According to a recent study by the American Association of Fund-Raising Counsel, Inc., charitable giving in America totaled $35.2 billion in 1977—an increase of almost $6 billion over the previous year. Individuals gave $29.5 billion or 83.8 percent of the total amount while bequests equaled $2.12 billion or 6 percent of the total. The remaining 10.2 percent was divided between foundations ($2.01 billion) and corporations ($1.57 billion).

Of the overall total, it is estimated that the area of civic and public affairs, which in this study included preservation, received about $1.09 billion in contributions from individuals, bequests, corporations and foundations in 1977. What are the problems and potential of each of these philanthropic groups?

A key problem facing all preservation groups is how to channel individual interest and potential financial support to specific projects and to promote greater financial stability for local, regional and national preservation organizations. It is a difficult task to harness financial commitment for preservation from individuals, particularly for general operating purposes. However, if a potential donor is well educated by the organization and called upon for specific participation in a project, a major gift commitment could be forthcoming. After all, as indicated above, individuals through their donations and bequests were the source of almost 90 percent of all charitable dollars in 1977.

Foundation philanthropy is a little easier to predict than an individual's giving pattern. Many of the more than 26,000 grant-making foundations in the United States have somewhat defined areas of interest, giving patterns and procedures for applying for available funds that have been determined by the donors or interpreted by the foundation's officers and trustees. Reference books published by the Foundation Center (*Foundation Directory, National Data Book* and *Source Book Profiles*. Distributed by Columbia

University Press) are particularly helpful in researching these numerous foundations.

Unfortunately, America's private industry has been slow in developing an interest in historic preservation. Until recently much of the business community believed that preservation was regressive. Now, however, this attitude is slowly beginning to change—especially since more substantive information on business involvement in preservation is being published and widely circulated. The INFORM study *New Profits from Old Buildings* (McGraw-Hill, 1978), which examined 71 preservation projects undertaken by companies throughout the United States, is helping to fill this information gap. But much more remains to be done to educate the country's corporate leaders about the aesthetic and economic benefits of historic preservation.

QUESTIONS TO BE CONSIDERED

In what ways could preservationists be more effective in gaining greater contributions from the corporate sector? How can unrestricted giving be increased to at least equal the gifts for specific programs and projects? Can preservation be marketed so as to elicit a generous response from skeptics?

PUBLIC TAX POLICY

The ramifications of tax law for preservation are pervasive. For example, tax laws profoundly affect the existence and solvency of private historic preservation organizations and the ability of the private sector in general to preserve, maintain and rehabilitate our legacy of significant structures. Virtually every kind of statutory tax and, in particular, the income, estate and property taxes come into play. With few exceptions, these laws traditionally have hindered historic preservation efforts and have belied the national commitment to preservation expressed in the National Historic Preservation Act of 1966 and elsewhere. The tax laws have encouraged new construction and the deterioration at best, or demolition at worst, of historically or architecturally significant structures. Nonprofit preservation organizations seeking to change this situation have had to act judiciously to avoid lobbying, which might endanger their tax exemptions and very existence.

In the past few years, however, new tax laws and changes in the interpretation of existing ones have made historic preservation much more viable than before. Section 2124 of the Tax Reform Act of 1976 has created incentives for the rehabilitation of historic commercial and other income-producing properties that have engendered nearly $350 million in rehabilitation work. The Revenue Act of 1978 recently added another incentive in its 10 percent investment tax credit for rehabilitating older buildings for commercial or industrial purposes. Preservation groups are freer to lobby and to expand the scope of their allowable tax-exempt activities through mechanisms such as revolving funds. States and localities, too, have joined this trend by enacting income and property tax relief measures for designated historic properties.

Despite this fairer shake now offered private preservation efforts by the tax laws, the agenda of public tax policy issues affecting historic preservation remains full. The existence of many historic houses and estates occupied as residences is threatened by weighty repair and maintenance costs, for which there is no tax relief. Estate taxes still force sale and/or subdivision of historic properties by taxing them based on their fair market ("highest and best use"), rather than current use, values. Most historic structures and districts still do not receive property tax relief, and laws enacted for this purpose have, in large part, not been properly publicized nor effectively utilized.

The section 2124 tax incentives expire in 1981, and the effort to reenact them may encounter opposition from reformers seeking to eliminate tax loopholes and preferences. Even now, the section 2124 disincentives to demolition and new construction have divided preservationists as to their value and aroused some public opposition. Section 2124 withdrew previously available tax deductions for expenses incurred in demolishing historic structures and limited the depreciation tax deductions available for new buildings constructed on their sites. Some preservationists believe these disincentives are too punitive. This reaction has been oc-

disincentives

casioned in part by public officials complaining that the disincentives will result in retaining all designated historic structures, whether economically viable or not, at the expense of new development projects that may arguably be more worthwhile. Some of these public officials are threatening to keep historic urban areas from being listed in the National Register of Historic Places in order to prevent the applicability of these tax disincentives. Consideration also should be given to restoring the originally enacted requirement that donations of partial interests in property, such as preservation easements, need be only 30 years in duration to get a tax deduction. Other new suggestions for consideration include a tax to discourage speculation in areas undergoing rehabilitation and tax incentives to encourage lending institutions to reinvest in urban historic areas.

QUESTIONS TO BE CONSIDERED

What should be the legislative priorities of the private sector in the field of tax law? What new incentives for preservation should be most strongly advocated by the private preservation sector? Should direct tax relief be sought for owner-occupied historic structures and, if so, in what form? What should preservationists say to the argument that historic preservation should be funded only through direct governmental grants? How can preservationists justify tax relief considering the current trend toward removing tax shelters?

PRIVATE FINANCIAL INSTITUTIONS AND REAL ESTATE DEVELOPERS

Private financial institutions, principally insurance companies, banks, savings and loans and real estate developers, are playing an increasing role in the preservation movement. Interest on the part of financial institutions results in part from federal and state antiredlining laws, corporate image building concerns and demonstrated interest and accomplishments of real estate developers. To some extent, both developers and institutions from which they seek financing have grown to view preservation as a profitable form of real estate development as a result of special tax incentives,

201

increased costs of new construction and consumer demand for space in old buildings. These institutions are currently involved in commercial and residential preservation development through both profit-making activities, such as loans and investments, and charitable initiatives, such as contributions, subsidies and volunteer efforts.

The relationship between private nonprofit preservation organizations and financial institutions and developers will become more important as their areas of preservation involvement expand. Each will benefit from sharing information and resources. Sometimes conflicts will arise between the for-profit and nonprofit sectors because of differences in their goals and values. Private nonprofit preservation organizations may gain from partnerships with for-profit institutions. They should define their own activities by determining what the private for-profit sector is unwilling or unable to do.

QUESTIONS TO BE CONSIDERED

How can nonprofit organizations encourage cooperation between private organizations and the public sector in order to finance preservation projects? How can nonprofit preservation groups assist the financial and development institutions in focusing on community goals and complying with state and federal regulations? What financial and management techniques can be adapted for use by private nonprofit organizations? How should nonprofit preservation groups participate in the social initiatives of the financial and development sector?

THE NONPROFIT SECTOR

Nonprofit organizations, sometimes called voluntary organizations or the "third sector" (the others being the public and private for-profit sectors), have played an important role in preservation since the earliest days of the movement. Most preservation organizations are nonprofits, ranging from small local historical societies to citywide, statewide and regional preservation organizations. Such organizations have been instrumental in educating their memberships and the public at large in preservation values and methodology and have been in many instances the primary spur to legislation and other public sector initiatives at the local, state and national levels. Recently, preservation nonprofits have widened the scope of their concerns and activities, becoming involved, for instance, in real estate development, merchandising programs, preservation loan programs and the supervision of preservation easements.

While it is easy to take for granted the role of nonprofits in preservation, it is important to recognize that they constitute a small part of the diverse third sector, which depends for its survival and well-being on tax laws and related legislation. Rulings by the Internal Revenue Service on what constitutes appropriate activities by tax-exempt organizations, legislation on lobbying by nonprofits and changes in the tax law itself will have a fundamental impact on the future of nonprofit organizations and on the role such organizations continue to have in historic preservation.

QUESTIONS TO BE CONSIDERED

Many questions confront the nonprofit sector, including whether or not it should contribute—and if so, how—to the organized efforts of the third sector to sustain and/or enlarge tax incentives for charitable activities. Should nonprofit preservation organizations be a more conspicuous presence in the institutional structures of the third sector? Should they seek to establish specified roles for themselves in carrying out preservation-related legislation? Should all nonprofit organizations elect to lobby and, if so, how should they coordinate their lobbying activities? Should the non-profit organizations develop objectives in order to avoid overlap with public and profit-making sectors? How can they develop more representative boards of trustees, committees and memberships?

NEIGHBORHOOD CONSERVATION

Several interrelated but separate neighborhood conservation movements are under way in the United States. Citizens in virtually every type of neighborhood, from suburb to inner city, are recognizing that they must organize to protect their collective interests. Community organizers work to organize low and moderate-income residents in deteriorating neighborhoods. City governments, aided by Community Development Block Grants, are undertaking a wide variety of neighborhood conservation programs. Preservation is closely identified with what is commonly called the back-to-the-city movement, which has relied on private capital and market forces for the dramatic revitalization of numerous older neighborhoods.

Preservationists, and the use of preservation techniques by "urban pioneers," have revolutionized the public perception of older neighborhoods. Badly deteriorated neighborhoods have become revitalized historic districts, protected by the National Register of Historic Places and by locally enacted historic district zoning.

Initially, the back-to-the-city movement was seen in a totally positive light, as a rearguard action against white flight and the rush to the suburbs. Today, however, the rush back to the city itself has become a major phenomenon, reinforced by such interrelated forces as high new housing costs, clogged freeways, the energy crisis and the entry of the baby boom generation into the housing market. As the movement grows, criticism also grows that this form of urban revitalization is directly and indirectly causing hardships for the poor, the elderly and minority groups.

The other organizations and agencies involved in neighborhood conservation have varied perceptions of preservation. Groups organized to aid low-income persons often view preservation as a threat, as part of a revitalization process that causes rising rents, higher taxes and displacement of neighborhood residents. Many neighborhood improvement societies do not consider their areas historic and do not see the relevance of preservation to them. Local governments have mixed views about preservation, viewing it as both an aid and a potential roadblock to their development plans.

QUESTIONS TO BE CONSIDERED

Neighborhood conservation and historic preservation are merging or diverging in their interests and techniques, depending on the source of information. But whichever view is put forward, it raises a basic question: Should neighborhood conservation be viewed as a major component of preservation or would it be better to view neighborhood conservation and preservation as allied, but separate endeavors? If the two are allied, should preservationists become concerned with the entire spectrum of issues that affect urban neighborhoods, such as schools, crime prevention, job opportunities, etc.? Can the techniques, experiences and contacts of preservation be used to help a wider array of neighborhoods? Should preservation develop more flexible techniques to work more effectively in "average" neighborhoods? Should preservation add to its other objectives the goal of maintaining neighborhood diversity—a mix of incomes, races, ethnic groups and ages? If this is a viable option, should preservationists then lobby for and support government housing programs, rent control and eviction control laws and tax relief measures to assist low and moderate-income residents? Is it advisable for preservationists to undertake government-assisted projects to aid low and moderate-income families while also achieving physical preservation objectives?

PRESERVATION AND CONSERVATION: A CONVERGENCE OF INTERESTS?

The 1973 report *Goals and Programs* (Study Committee Report to the Board of Trustees, National Trust for Historic

205

Preservation) recommended that the National Trust assume a role in preserving America's "historic and cultural landscape." The study noted that there was no national program directed toward preserving America's rural landscape. Today, the National Trust is embarked on a three-year project to promote rural preservation.

The only national environmental organization that has focused concern on protecting natural rural as well as urban areas is the Conservation Foundation. Most others have limited their concerns to wilderness areas. The Sierra Club recently has shown an interest in urban conservation in addition to its traditional concern for wilderness but evidences less interest in the rural areas that fall between the wilderness and the city. Other organizations such as the National Rural Center, the National Association of Conservation Districts and the American Land Forum are interested in rural land issues, particularly prime farmland retention.

At the state and local levels there are few organizations that show a combined concern for historic preservation and open space protection. Examples of those that do are the French and Pickering Creeks Conservation Trust, Pa.; the Piedmont Environmental Council, Va.; the Catskill Center, N.Y.; Massachusetts Trustees of Reservations; and the Maine Coast Heritage Trust.

It is interesting to note that in England, in sharp contrast to the United States, both government and private organizations traditionally have shown a combined interest in preservation and open space protection.

QUESTIONS TO BE CONSIDERED

To what extent should preservationists concern themselves with open space protection? Should they combine forces with environmentalists? Are the traditional private sector preservation techniques such as easements and revolving funds effective in dealing with rural preservation problems? Rural preservation organizations should seek to gain broad public support in their communities. To do so, they must ask how effective is cooperation between rural preservationists and local government. Can rural preservationists do more to promote local ordinance controls? Rural preservation organizations should analyze where their financial support comes from today and where it might come from in the future. Do the local private preservation organizations need assistance from national organizations in developing effective rural preservation programs. If so, in what areas? Would the techniques used by environmental organizations, such as the Nature Conservancy and the Trust for Public Land, be helpful?

PRESERVATION'S BACKLASHES

Proponents of historic preservation and neighborhood conservation have assumed increasing power in determining future directions for cities and towns throughout the nation. While preservation and preservationists were regarded only as irritants to "progress" in the past, changing public attitudes supported by a growing body of federal, state and local legislation provide new opportunities to preserve historic properties.

Success and power often breed new problems. Older neighborhoods provide affordable single-family dwellings with the prospect of appreciated value for reinvesting in older houses. The back-to-the-city movement is accused of reducing the supply of adequate housing for low and moderate-income groups and of displacing existing neighborhood residents. Opportunities to use the National Register of Historic Places and the preservation provisions of the Tax Reform Act of 1976, while providing development incentives for investors, can also be used to discourage unwanted new development projects. Given the broad criteria for the National Register of Historic Places, antidevelopment forces sometimes attempt to place properties of marginal significance in the National Register of Historic Places as either last-ditch obstacles to new development or as a justification for mediocre projects.

Increased emphasis on the reuse of older buildings has resulted in expanded rehabilitation of city halls, libraries, post offices and other public buildings. These structures are not easily equipped to meet the needs of the physically handicapped. Advocates of barrier-free access accuse preservationists of insensitivity to human problems, which they see as more important than preservation "purity."

A decade ago, preservationists promoted the restoration of historic buildings and districts as an economic boon to communities through increased tourism. Today, residents in restored and rehabilitated communities are resisting an ever-expanding tourist industry that affects their own right to privacy. Tourism also generates the development of hotels, motels and fast-food establishments that detract from the appearance of the community.

Many still see preservation as an elitist effort; although its orientation has changed from a preoccupation with historic house museums, it is nonetheless considered a vocation or avocation for a limited segment of the population. Even though the preservation movement's participants and concerns are increasingly diverse, there is an increasing backlash, justified or unjustified, against preservation when it comes into conflict with other important national, state and local social, economic and political goals.

QUESTIONS TO BE CONSIDERED

Has the growth of the preservation movement caused it to extend itself beyond legitimate boundaries? Has historic preservation become a source of social and economic displacement or is it used as a scapegoat for other sources of displacement? Is the nomination process for inclusion in the National Register of Historic Places abused? Are current methods adequate for determining whether preservation, or some other development alternative, provides for the greater public good? Is the movement as elitist today as it was in the past or was that a distorted perception? What are the proper limits of modification to historic buildings to meet the requirements of the handicapped and the aged?

PATTERNS IN ORGANIZING FOR PRESERVATION: LOCAL

The past decade has witnessed a proliferation of organized preservation activities at the local level. Sometimes the

208

impetus for action comes from a long-established historical society that expands its perceived mandate. More often, however, the preservation organization is a spin-off or entirely new group, formed in response to an immediate threat, then broadened in purpose.

Whether encouraged by municipal officials or in response to their less-than-sensitive policies, the private sector has discovered that only through collective efforts can preservation be widely effective. Thus, more preservationists are awakening to the need for greater political and social leadership involvement and for forming alliances with other causes such as housing, transportation, energy and education—one reason why, although the volunteer role is still quite strong, more and more organizations are professionally staffed.

Depending on the level of sophistication and availability of resources, local preservation groups have conducted surveys, drafted preservation ordinances, supported commissions, performed feasibility studies, developed educational programs and even entered the real estate market through revolving funds. In the process, preservationists have been quick to embrace and use to immediate advantage such instruments as the National Register of Historic Places and historic district ordinances. Often, however, this has been done before the values of preservation have been thoroughly instilled in the community, resulting in backlash when the inevitable challenges to the power structure and/or growth occur. Part of the trouble stems from the fact that, unlike other established civic causes such as the United Fund, hospitals, colleges and youth activities, preservation does not always attract the involvement of top community leadership. Conflicts between the old guard, newcomers and highly motivated individuals will continue to be an important element in the next decade. Other problems may result from such sources as the disincentives of the Tax Reform Act of 1976, since their full implications are seldom presented in preservationists' campaigns for listing a property in the National Register of Historic Places.

Local organizations should determine how best to respond to the need for a deep community acceptance of the preservation ethic and develop programs to respond to this need. What support should they expect from state and national organizations in this respect? Can local organizations broaden their outlooks to enlarge their base of support among all socioeconomic groups? Should local organizations be volunteer oriented or should they hire professional staff? How can they develop stronger leadership within the community to insure continuity?

PATTERNS IN ORGANIZING FOR PRESERVATION: STATE

Traditionally, state public programs have concerned the ownership of major historic properties and the support of state historical societies. The current major public contributions to preservation have been those associated with the administration of the National Register of Historic Places programs through the state historic preservation offices. Because of the requirements placed on state historic preservation offices to complete state surveys, administer the matching grants-in-aid program and participate in the federally mandated A-95 review process, little time has been available to address broader preservation planning issues, through advocacy or through innovation, in land-use related policy and programs. Until recently, the private sector's efforts in historic preservation have been focused on nurturing the development of legislative policy and funding programs at the local, state and federal levels.

Recognizing that the states possess constitutional control over the structure and legal power of local government and increasingly assume the key role in the administration of all federally assisted or required planning programs, private preservationists have organized to initiate, coordinate, supplement and advocate the influence of the state's public preservation activities. Some private state historic preservation organizations have been formed as a result of legislative action. However, most of these groups are incorporated and structured in a way similar to other privately supported 501(c)(3) organizations active in preservation. Interpretations of program policy emphases and organizational capacity vary widely based on decisions by the organization's governing body as to the type and level of input necessary at the state level to affect preservation.

Program and staff commitments range from the unstaffed, volunteer committee-based organizations producing and disseminating information through newsletters and conferences or special events to those staffed organizations that engage in various program combinations of advocacy, technical assistance, information exchange, planning consultancy, lobbying or the operation of a revolving fund for real estate development or financial assistance purposes.

QUESTIONS TO BE CONSIDERED

State groups should consider the relationship of their organizations to private and public local and national organizations, and they should define who is or should be served by them. Is there a need to coordinate the regional or national interests and activities of private state organizations? Sources of support should be considered—membership, fee-based services and annual grants from the state historic preservation offices. How should private preservation organizations work with state preservation offices for financial support?

PATTERNS IN ORGANIZING
FOR PRESERVATION: NATIONAL

Since 1966 there has been rapid growth in the number of national, private, nonprofit preservation organizations. Older organizations such as the American Association for State and Local History, American Association of Museums and the National Trust have seen their memberships grow in number and have, in some instances, structured their governing and advisory bodies toward a regionalized system. Professional organizations have moved toward creation of new, or expansion of existing, organizational networks to better serve regions and states. Professional and scholarly organizations have expanded their preservation-related committees and involvements, such as the American Institute of Architects' Committee on Historic Resources and the Society of Architectural Historians' Historic Preservation Committee. New national organizations have come into being to serve special areas of concern to preservationists, including the Friends of Cast-Iron Architecture, Society for Industrial Archeology, National Center for Preservation Law, Preservation Action, Victorian Society in America and the Historic House Association of America.

QUESTIONS TO BE CONSIDERED

National organizations should consider how their expansion in number is perceived by individuals and organizations working at the local level. Is the trend toward more national organizations related to special facets of preservation going to continue? Is there an effective means of communication among the groups to make their individual efforts known and available? Is there an unrecognized and unnecessary program competition between groups? If there is, does this impede the economic survival and growth of national groups?

PUBLISHING FOR PRESERVATION

Communication is a cornerstone of preservation, and publications are key tools in communicating both the idea and the information of preservation. The concept "publish or perish" is especially pertinent for preservation. Without creating popular support and general understanding of its purposes and techniques, preservation's future cannot be assured. Publishing means more than just making things available; it means "to broadcast," choosing and disseminating information according to a plan. Even in this electronic age of television, radio, film and video-recorders, media experts have proven the fallacy of the supposition that telecommunications would displace print media. The differences in the two media create audiences for each type of communication. Publications have been called the "medium of continuity—the medium of history. . . . Television may have become our eyes and ears and our public meeting place, but print continues to be our memory." (*The New Yorker*, October 2, 1978).

Among their attributes, publications share with old buildings a number of special characteristics: They are not readily disposable; they are cost-effective and useful; they provide for greater freedom of expression and diversity; they last, in memory and form. In particular, publications provide the only feasible form for transmittal of certain information, e.g., technical information that requires careful review and retention for future consultation. Publications are also the only financially feasible means of communicating with small audiences—between professional preservationists as well as between preservationists and their public.

Preservationist publishers are finding that publications are one of the most effective, and often the only, means of keeping in touch with increasingly diverse and dispersed memberships. They are finding that publications offer a feasible opportunity for creating a unique public image through use of a unified design image and editorial approach. Publications such as books (e.g., local architectural surveys), guidebooks, even calendars and notecards, are being used to create operating revenues for their sponsoring organizations; other groups sell preservation publications of outside publishers as an additional income source. Publications are a proven means of logically communicating the preservation message.

Publications have helped build a strong communications network among preservationists and continue to serve as a prime link in that effort. Publishers of preservation information today include private preservation groups at local, state and national levels; government agencies at all levels; preservation-related organizations; trade publishers; university presses; and the commercial print media (magazines and newspapers). Preservation publishing is steadily increasing, as evidenced by the several hundred local organizations with active newsletters, more ambitious publishing programs, trade interest in preservation-related books and the number of new government preservation publications.

The growth of preservation publishing demands that standards of accuracy, effectiveness and design be maintained to avoid duplication of subject. Cooperative ventures between commercial publishers and preservationists would ease the problems confronted by small organizations in publishing, distributing, promoting and in selecting subjects for publication.

QUESTIONS TO BE CONSIDERED

In what ways can publications be used more to interest and inform the public about preservation? What should be the role of publications in an overall communications strategy for preservation? Is there a way in which national preservation publishing priorities can be established, independently as now, or in a more systematic and coordinated manner? Should responsibility for preparing and publishing technical preservation publications be centralized? If so, at what level and in which organizations? How can additional sources of publications funding be developed? How can publications be developed to yield revenue to support preservation activities?

USE OF THE MEDIA

The preservation movement has made important strides in dealing effectively with the media, especially the print media. Evidence of this is revealed in scanning clips of preservation stories appearing in newspapers and magazines throughout the country. For example, as recently as five years ago the number of preservation news stories appearing in one week was roughly 100; today the total is close to 500 per week.

Moreover, major national news outlets such as *Newsweek*, *Business Week* and NBC-TV have covered preservation in a substantive manner, dealing with the subject as a movement rather than merely reporting on isolated cases of restored buildings, as is often the case. The media's preference for conflicts frequently leads to sensationalized and sometimes overly simplistic reporting of complex issues. All too often, preservation battles on the local level are conflicts between strong factions—preservationists versus real estate developers and city hall, and sometimes even preservationists versus preservationists.

And yet, despite wider media coverage, preservation is still only vaguely understood. Many reporters working for national magazines or important daily newspapers seem only mildly, if at all, interested in preservation. This is particularly true of the business and financial press, an important group to reach if the business world is to be convinced of the economic benefits of preservation.

Clearly, much work lies ahead in aggressive public relations planning and programming if preservation is to capture the attention of the mass media as the conservation movement did a decade or so ago. Use might be made of outside professional public relations agencies or consultants to communicate to the media the preservation point of view. Forming loose coalitions of national, state and local preservation organizations also would make possible a coordinated approach to the media. Consideration should be given to advocacy advertising as another means of educating the public about the importance of preservation to the nation's quality of life.

While there is no question that effective and widespread media coverage can provide direct benefits to preservation,

215

there are serious pitfalls to be avoided. By following on the heels of the environmental movement, preservation is in a unique spot to take advantage of some important lessons learned by the environmentalists. Many news stories have positioned environmentalists as "anti-everything"—antigrowth, antinuclear, anticoal. Careful public relations planning is required on the part of preservationists to overcome being labeled in such negative terms.

QUESTIONS TO BE CONSIDERED

How can preservationists effectively use the media to shape a consistent, appropriate image—one in keeping with the movement's new directions? How can the preservation movement best use the media to exploit the support evident at the local level to enhance growth of this grass-roots participation throughout the country? How can preservationists avoid the pitfall of being labeled as "obstructionists" or "antiprogress" by the media? Should preservationists be willing to compromise on a local, regional or national issue to soften the appearance of caring more for buildings than for people, being unrealistic in goals and demanding more than is economically or otherwise prudent? How can preservationists encourage and support the media's recent efforts to treat preservation as a national movement having economic, aesthetic, cultural and quality-of-life implications to gain more in-depth coverage?

PRESERVATION EDUCATION: STUDENT PERSPECTIVES

The student population involved in preservation education ranges in age and goals from elementary schoolchildren engaged in learning about the neighborhood surrounding the school building to the seasoned professional seeking a training program that will provide background on new legislation that affects preservation work. What differentiates the student needs in education from those of the general public is the formal, structured and selective approach of the educational process.

There are two goals of formal education in preservation.

One goal is general awareness, appreciation and commitment to preservation among individuals who will support preservation efforts but who are not involved as full-time professionals. This objective is most commonly associated with the primary and secondary school population and, to a lesser extent, with those colleges and universities that now sponsor individual courses in preservation. The second goal of formal education is career-oriented. This objective is embraced by the degree programs in preservation currently sponsored by colleges and universities. Professional development also is the objective of the many shorter and nondegree training programs and educational opportunities available to practicing professionals involved in design, historical or other work related to preservation. These shorter training and educational opportunities also are available to active volunteers who exercise influence in their communities.

By category, preservation education's concerns are:

Elementary and secondary school programs—integrating preservation-related material into the required curriculum for history, math, science, English, etc.

Higher education programs—developing and expanding core and elective subject material for individual courses and degree programs sponsored by schools or departments of architecture, law, planning, history, business, anthropology, landscape architecture, etc.

Continuing education and training programs—increasing the number of short and individual courses offered by colleges, universities, organizations and agencies for professionals, paraprofessionals, active volunteers and the general public.

Internships—increasing the number of internships sponsored by colleges and universities in cooperation with organizations and agencies as well as those sponsored independently by organizations and agencies.

Program enrichment—developing more community education programs, field trips, publications, specialized libraries, research opportunities to be offered by colleges and universities, often in cooperation with organizations and agencies, to reinforce commitment to community service and to maintain knowledge of actual work in the field.

At the primary and secondary school levels, should programs be oriented toward activities separate from the regular required academic curricula or should they be developed to be easily integrated into regular teaching materials? In view of the "back-to-the-basics" movement in education, how can preservation programs be made attractive to teachers and school administrators? At the college level, a major question is how private preservation organizations can work better with students and professors associated with preservation courses or degree programs to their mutual benefit. Can the private sector determine the needs of the field in order to guide the development of preservation courses and degree programs? How can professionals, active volunteers and the general public learn about continuing education and training programs available to them? How can internship opportunities be better organized to provide the work experience necessary for employment in the field as well as to assure equal benefit to the sponsoring organization?

PRESERVATION EDUCATION: PRIVATE AND PUBLIC

Until the 1960s, any formal education of those involved in the historic preservation movement was provided by traditional undergraduate and graduate degree programs in history, architecture, archeology and library studies. Few colleges stressed preservation as a career option, and most graduates who engaged in preservation activity did so as an adjunct to their work as historical agency administrators, historians, researchers, librarians, museum curators, archeologists and architects.

Because most historical agencies that engaged in preservation educational activity were local or regional nonprofit organizations, their efforts were directed primarily at sensitizing their members and local citizens to the importance of local history, the value of preservation and the promotion of civic pride and historical participation. The

218

most educationally active of the state historical associations have been those in the East and Midwest. Most state and local educational efforts in the past have been concerned solely with broadening public awareness.

Following World War II the rising demand for educational programs to develop lay expertise and professional training in preservation was met by private state and national history groups, architectural history groups, preservation organizations and, more recently, by colleges and universities. In the past 15 years the growth has been significant. Today, more than 20 colleges and universities offer degree programs in preservation and nearly 200 others offer individual courses in aspects of preservation. Professional conferences, publications, books, research projects and internships have increased in equally dramatic fashion.

Public agency involvement in preservation education has been concerned mainly with training public employees. Significant programs were initiated in the 1930s in the interpretation of historic houses and sites for the general public. More recently public agency educational efforts have been made by some federal and state preservation agencies and as a result of recent legislation. Some are tending toward the development of research projects, publications and training programs for private sector preservationists as well.

A number of local preservation organizations have endeavored to develop preservation curriculum materials for use in local primary and secondary schools.

QUESTIONS TO BE CONSIDERED

What are the educational priorities of preservation that should be served by the private sector and by the public sector? How should these two sectors work with primary and secondary schools? Should universities be encouraged to provide more of the educational and research needs of the field? How can duplication of effort be avoided in educational efforts sponsored by the private and public sectors? Should opportunities in mid-career or short course training for professionals be expanded? If so, what areas are in need of attention? Can educational programs in preservation be helped by technology, e.g., videotape cassettes and computers?

PRESERVATION INFORMATION

Both the knowledge of and access to information are necessary for the preservation activities supported by private individuals and organizations. In the effort to rehabilitate, restore, revitalize and reuse a three-dimensional environment, preservationists rely on two-dimensional documents. There is a growing recognition that we must be responsible for documenting and preserving the history of the preservation movement. The collection and use of information on preservation encourages further research that then can be added in a cyclical manner to the store of knowledge. It also aids in defining and recognizing this multidisciplinary field of study.

Partially because access to information is thought to be one of the inalienable rights provided by our government, private organizations usually are reluctant to add it to the cost of their overhead. It often is difficult to prove the value of research in terms of income and profit. Costs are involved in collecting, organizing, preserving and distributing preservation information. Such information includes audiovisual, archival, computer output, printed books and periodicals and microreduced materials.

Currently, the major repositories of preservation information are at universities, such as the Avery Architectural Library at Columbia University; federal government agencies, such as the U.S. Department of the Interior; and national private organizations, such as the National Trust.

Private organizations that produce and often collect preservation information can be divided into the following categories:

1. National groups with a special interest, such as the Society for Industrial Archeology, and allied professional groups, such as the National Association of Housing and Redevelopment Officials.

2. Statewide private preservation groups, such as the Preservation League of New York State.

3. Regional private preservation groups, such as the Landmark Society of Western New York and the Society for the Preservation of New England Antiquities.

4. Local groups, such as museums, historical societies,

220

civic groups and private urban preservation groups.

5. Educational institutions with preservation programs.

The task of identifying and locating all potential preservation information is enormous. In the search for information, the preservationist must go to organizations that neither produce nor retain records for the purpose of research. Examples are churches that keep genealogical or historical records, municipal agencies that keep census records, county agencies that keep property information, governmental organizations that keep archival information, architects' offices that keep working drawings. Because preservation can include such a broad range of activities, almost any organizational or individual collection potentially includes relevant information.

QUESTIONS TO BE CONSIDERED

Is further access to preservation information needed? What kinds of information resources would support and encourage further private preservation activities at the local level? Is it feasible to locate all preservation information in a given locality and encourage its administrators to make that information accessible to those working on preservation projects? How can private preservationists encourage the collection and recognition of preservation information in public and academic libraries? Should private groups be responsible for collecting the resources produced by their organizations? How can they make others aware of what is available from their organization?

DEFINING CONTEMPORARY PRESERVATION

As the preservation movement has grown in numbers and professionalization, a special language of preservation has evolved along with it. In creating their own jargon, preservationists have called on the languages of architecture, urban planning, law, conservation, archeology, design, history, museum work, finance, real estate development, community activism and America's ethnic heritages. There exists no common preservation vocabulary. There is much public confusion over basic preservation terms such as the difference between "restoration" and "rehabilitation," "preservation" and "rehabilitation" and "preservation" and "conservation"; furthermore, such words are used differently among preservationists themselves.

There have been a few official attempts to define preservation terminology, notably by the Heritage Conservation and Recreation Service (HCRS) and the National Conservation Advisory Council, but these efforts were restricted to selected basic preservation terms. HCRS also has defined selected economic terms for use in its Tax Reform Act of 1976 certification process. Such definitions are helpful in setting ascertainable standards for certification, tax benefits and applicability to specific federal programs, but they are necessarily limited in scope.

Private efforts are varied. While many authoritative architectural dictionaries exist, only a few can be found with definitions for such terms as zoning, open space, urban planning, real estate and mortgage banking. The few environmental glossaries that have been published relate primarily to scientific and technical terminology for energy and natural conservation. Efforts in defining terminology in the field of architectural conservation are especially barren, the only glossary being the *Glossarium Artis* series (published in German, French and English) and one published by the Canadian Museum Association. In response to the need for more uniform preservation definitions, the National Trust is compiling *Landmark Words,* a glossary of 3,000 terms drawn from preservation and related disciplines.

A common language to communicate the ideas underlying preservation and to speak clearly and understand this language is a need not only of professional preservationists but of all who become involved: volunteers who must understand the built environment in order to describe it in architectural surveys; students and educators in preservation courses; public officials required to gauge the environmental impact of their decisions; attorneys and legislators who work with preservation laws; bankers and developers, etc. But defining preservation's words is only a first step in developing a common vocabulary. The test of its effectiveness will be in how this language is used to communicate preservation concepts. In that sense, defining the language of preservation can be a foundation of the entire preservation effort.

QUESTIONS TO BE CONSIDERED

Is development of a preservation terminology a realistic goal? If so, who should be responsible for defining preservation—should the public and private sectors be a part of the process? Is a uniform language possible or desirable? Would the uniformity required for official purposes impede the flexibility required for growth, change and varied users? Can consistency be promoted among federal, state, local, public and private efforts? How does preservation terminology affect the public's perception of preservation? Are there negative images that result from this terminology? Is it possible for the technical terminology of building restoration to mix with the popular language of the preservation movement? Is there a danger that preservation language may become so refined that preservationists will not be understood by the public?

PRESERVATION AND THE PLANNING PROCESS

How should preservation be integrated into the planning process? The National Historic Preservation Act of 1966 mandates the preparation of comprehensive statewide preservation plans. Some states have begun integrating preservation elements in their planning programs. At the local level, only planning for land use has really made any progress. The current state of the art appears to be an increasingly complex system of balancing different interests with ever-expanding rules and regulations administered by bureaucratized staff and commissions. The process becomes alienating and mystifying through increasingly technical bases and findings for making decisions and by growing reliance on experts or professionals for information.

Preservationists should look to the environmentalists' experience in the past decade. Environmental legislation and administration are prime examples of political trade-offs and an increasingly complex set of rules and regulations. Long-term, consistent pressure is still crucial in advocating a position in keeping with the spirit of the original intent. Even with a broadening public interest and awareness of its purposes, the environmental movement constantly faces new pressures from its former opponents and from the bureaucratic process. Will preservation have better success?

Preservation, at least the connotation it holds in the mind of the general public and public officials, may enter the planning process with even less of a competitive position than former environmental activities. Enormous popular energy will still be necessary to assure any success through interminable hearings and regulatory procedures. Supporters may be less willing to follow up on an apparent victory once preservation is integrated into the planning process. Turning the preservation planning reins over to professionals and politicians should be an issue carefully considered by preservationists. A conscious and deliberate evolution of both planning and the preservation movement will be necessary to assure a democratic and comprehensive planning process.

QUESTIONS TO BE CONSIDERED

What areas of planning might be considered targets for influencing a preservation component? What weight does preservation carry in decisions concerning planning? Does preservation exhibit any deficiencies that lessen its import? With what other issue-oriented groups might preservationists form alliances to carry more weight for their cause?

PROPERTY STEWARDSHIP

The fundamental purpose of all preservation programs is to assure the retention of those properties that are considered, by responsible authorities and thoughtful persons, worth keeping as part of the national heritage. These properties are regarded as valuable because they remind us of our nation's achievements, enrich our daily lives by their presence and teach us lessons that may guide or inspire future actions. The reasons why property may be considered worth keeping have increased considerably in the past 50 years, with recognition that a society or culture is represented by more than the singular places associated with prominent persons or great events. Historic districts, large estates, main streets, industrial and commercial sites and regional landscapes are protected by preservationists today. Equally important is the implied shift away from publicly owned properties that serve mainly as museums to a much wider range of privately owned historic property that continues its original use or has been adapted for new purposes.

A great deal of attention has been devoted in recent years to developing ways to save threatened or neglected historic property. However, far less interest has been shown in what must be done about the equally crucial matter of maintaining physically and financially a historic property over the long term, once the immediate issue of saving it has been resolved successfully. It appears that the preservation movement has established itself firmly in the United States and that more and more properties may be saved in the future. Thus, it is time for preservationists to reexamine the concept of property stewardship and to clearly define what should be done, both to keep historic properties at recognized levels of professional standards and to see that they continue as viable elements in a contemporary society.

QUESTIONS TO BE CONSIDERED

Is it reasonable to expect federal, state or local governments to enact laws that would confer legal or economic benefits to private owners of historic property? If it is reasonable, what should be the extent of these sanctions? What are the most feasible approaches for conservation with respect to the several types of historic properties: the single structure or object, the large estate, the historic distirct and the regional landscape? Should historic properties be exempt from laws intended to assure public health, safety or equal opportunity if these laws require changes to historical materials or the original configuration of a property? In the operation of a historic property, what are the minimum standards for the care, improvement and interpretation of the property? What skills are needed by both volunteers and professionals to administer and maintain a property? Economics are of increasing concern for historic properties, raising the question of what kinds of income-promoting measures the owner of a historic property may undertake without jeopardizing the historical qualities that are intended to be preserved. When is it considered permissible to demolish historic property, and what are the guidelines for doing so? What is the relationship of archeological investigation at historic properties to the properties themselves, their preservation and interpretation?

ENDANGERED BUILDING TYPES

Changing economic and social conditions have endangered a wide variety of building types. Old inner-city churches and synagogues, for instance, face abandonment or demolition as their congregations move to the suburbs; movie theaters of the 1930s and 1940s are disappearing from our cities, victims of the same shift to the suburbs and the lure of television; older school buildings are the first to be closed in response to the continuing decline in the school-age population. Obsolete facilities, high maintenance costs and pressures for development, among other factors, have helped add breweries and banks, mansions and factories, railroad stations and barns to the endangered list. Buildings off the beaten track often are overlooked.

Certain types of endangered buildings have been the subject of studies and publications. In 1976, for example, the National Trust published *A Courthouse Conservation Handbook* in cooperation with the National Clearinghouse for Criminal Justice Planning and Architecture, to focus attention on the threat to older courthouses that are considered inadequate to meet the expanded needs of county governments. The technical leaflet "Solutions for Surplus Schools," recently published by the Preservation League of New York State, is based on a year-long study of the adaptive use possibilities of four such schools. *Reusing Railroad Stations, Book Two,* by the Educational Facilities Laboratories, provides information on the economics of adapting railroad stations to new uses.

Similarly, the League of Historic American Theatres has identified historic theaters throughout the country and encouraged efforts to preserve and reuse them. The Cheswick Center sponsored a conference in 1975 on alternative uses of church property, the proceedings of which were summarized in *The Challenge of Underused Church Properties and the Search for Alternatives.* The National Trust undertook a three-year Main Street Project, designed to provide guidelines for the economic revitalization of older downtown business areas in small and medium-sized towns and to encourage the preservation and restoration of the 19th and early 20th-century commercial buildings that line main streets throughout the country.

Because of changing conditions in our society, the list of endangered building types is expanding to include structures such as hotels, post offices, downtown department stores and jails. In view of this, it is important for preservationists to anticipate what types of buildings might be endangered in the future, as well as to understand the current scope of the problem.

As more and more buildings become endangered, consideration should be given to what resources (technical, legal, financial) are available to help in efforts to save them. Should studies be made of which major building types are likely to become endangered within the next few years and whether preservation organizations can anticipate problems in regard to certain building types? Are guidelines necessary? Can guidelines be developed for procedures involved in saving endangered buildings? What part can the private sector play in responding to the problem of endangered buildings? And how can national, statewide and local efforts be coordinated? Is adaptive use a solution?

PRESERVATION AS AN AVOCATION

Throughout its history, the American preservation movement has been largely the domain of individuals whose preservation-related activities have been avocational in nature. These individuals have formed the backbone of the preservation community. Their activities have been and continue to be varied: conducting tours of historic houses, organizing to save endangered landmarks, carrying out do-it-yourself renovation projects and securing the enactment of preservation legislation.

The very success of the nonprofessional preservation community in awakening public interest in conservation of the built environment and in lobbying for the passage of significant preservation legislation has stimulated a demand for greater technical skills in a field that has become increasingly complex. In response to this demand, the ranks of professional preservationists have swelled dramatically in recent years. With university programs turning out more professionally trained preservationists every year, and with increasing numbers of professionals in other fields—law, architecture and planning, to name only a few—turning to preservation as a full-time vocation, this increase in the professionalization of the field seems likely to continue. This fact, in turn, has led to something of a dilemma in the minds of both professionals and nonprofessionals. Professionals are sometimes critical or disdainful of the activities of those who "dabble" in preservation, while nonprofessionals are frustrated by the increasing sophistication of a field that they have helped to nurture for so long.

QUESTIONS TO BE CONSIDERED

Are there activities that should be the domain of the non-professional and others that should be the domain of the professional? Should the National Trust or other national or regional organizations have a responsibility to provide support to the nonprofessional or should such organizations concentrate their support and encouragement in the professional area? Do nonprofessionals have particular skills or assets to offer preservation and, if so, are they used to the fullest extent possible? What are the needs of nonprofessional preservationists? Are they met at the local, regional and national level?

PRESERVATION AS A VOCATION

Individuals have worked side by side on an amateur and professional basis from the beginning of the preservation movement in the United States. Volunteer boards work with paid staffs in the private, nonprofit sector and, in the public sector, appointed review board and commissions serve with the assistance of paid staff.

The distinction between professional and volunteer usually has been based on the combination of expertise and compensation. In preservation, volunteers often have as much knowledge and training as staff, particularly in the public sector where the qualifications for membership on review boards and commissions are set out in laws and regulations. The distinction between those working vocationally and avocationally is made on the basis of whether or not an individual is compensated. The term "vocation" is appropriate because it includes those working at professional and occupational levels in the field.

In the late 1960s, discussion arose on the subject of preservation as a profession. The combination of increased economic support for preservation and the concomitant demand for trained personnel brought this about. People working in the field for compensation, at a professional level, began to be described as preservationists.

A growing number of people are interested in working in preservation as the field has expanded and become economically more attractive. The desire to limit access to individuals who evidence proper training and experience comes about in order to create standards by which work can be judged. An example is the employment qualifications set out by the U.S. Department of the Interior's Heritage Conservation and Recreation Service for the staffs of the state historic preservation offices.

Because preservation projects have increased in number and complexity, there is a need to protect the structures and issues being worked on from incompetent individuals. Academic programs at the graduate level were developed primarily to meet the demand for trained personnel. This also has stimulated the desire to define the field as a profession.

QUESTIONS TO BE CONSIDERED

The needs of public and private preservation groups for trained professionals should be considered as well as the economic future of those employed in preservation. Whose concern should these factors be? Is there a need for criteria to be developed for judging a person's competency to work in preservation? Should professionals working in preservation be defined as "preservationists"?

SCHOLARSHIP IN PRESERVATION

Scholarship is the highest goal of academic study. But if scholarship is perceived by preservationists, as it often is by others, as "ivory tower" intellectualism, then preservationists are undermining their own existence, for the study of history is one of the quintessential exercises of the scholar.

Within the more narrow confines of preservation's educational programs, scholarship has been an elusive ideal.

230

Preservationists are being shortsighted in believing that scholarship must be limited to playing pedantic word games or producing lengthy erudite footnotes. To perpetuate this potentially debilitating posture is a mistake. Instead, primary research, archival investigation and historical analysis in preservation programs should be increased. A part of this effort should be defining precisely what is historic about historic preservation, a subject that needs a more systematic approach; scholarship could contribute significantly to this task.

Perhaps scholarship in preservation has not been widespread because scholars have not been invited to participate. Preservationists with sound academic credentials may not be in a position, because of programmatic or budgetary constraints, to take advantage of the scholars and their intellectual pursuits. But as the movement expands, time for the disciplined reflection and thoughtful contemplation of scholarship must be sought, encouraged and strongly supported by preservationists.

The history of America, from architecture to zoology, is essential to the informed preservationist. Preservationists of today are better and more skillfully trained, largely because of efforts on the college and university levels to educate and inform. Preservationists should be encouraged to increase their participation in the classroom and lecture hall. Also, seeking closer ties with professional institutions such as the College Art Association, Society of Architectural Historians and American Historical Association and encouraging professional seminars and meetings cannot help but benefit the preservation movement. The great resources of academic publishing should be strenuously sought out. Thoroughly researched papers, lectures, articles, books, etc., cannot help but have a positive effect on advancing the preservation movement.

QUESTIONS TO BE CONSIDERED

Can the tools of scholarship—research and writing—be of any value in broadening the foundation of the preservation movement to include all segments of American society? Should research projects that are corollaries to the announced goals of the preservation movement be encouraged and increased in the future? Would the advice of social scientists or historians help change the often reflexive, crisis-oriented image of the preservation movement? Could the technical assistance and educational aspirations of the preservation movement benefit from the scholar's knowledge and experience? Is it possible for the traditional house museum to become a broader-based research center? Should the preservation movement continue to rely on internal publishing mechanisms to reach potentially larger national audiences with scholarly publications?

PRIVATE ROLE IN DEVELOPING PUBLIC REGULATIONS

Many private sector preservationists recognize that it is necessary to support the passage of legislation beneficial to preservation interests on an ever-broadening range of subjects. Fewer consider that, once enacted, legislation usually is followed by implementing regulations that provide the detailed framework for carrying out legislative mandates.

Within the federal government, the agency implementing the legislative directive publishes proposed regulations in the *Federal Register*, and comments on them are accepted for a prescribed period of time. States have procedures similar in nature and purpose. At the local level, particularly with regard to building code practices and zoning matters, important opportunities exist for private participation in the development of public regulations.

The formal comment process and other means of participating in regulation development or revision afford private preservation organizations an opportunity to influence the actual implementation of legislation or regulatory authority that affects them, either by seeing that any necessary safeguards for historic properties are included or by assuring that preservation-related projects benefit as broadly as possible from a given program. Often, agencies or regulatory authorities are uncertain how best to write those portions of their regulations pertaining to preservation. Commentators can suggest language for inclusion that will meet preservation needs and objectives.

The comment process may lead to an ongoing dialogue between preservation and agency or regulatory authority representatives, resulting in increased understanding of and sensitivity to historic preservation. And, in the case of specific assistance programs, resulting familiarity of public entities with a private preservation group may benefit the group later should it seek assistance under that program. To date, few private preservation organizations below the national level have utilized the comment process as a vehicle for influencing assistance programs or regulatory authorities.

Regulations affect a wide range of preservation concerns from handicapped access to assistance programs. Assurance is necessary on certain aspects:

Handicapped accessibility—that historic buildings are altered only as a last resort and that waivers prevent impairment of significant property.

Energy—that caution is needed in applying energy conservation techniques or performance standards to historic properties.

Building and life safety codes—that code provisions do not make impossible or too expensive the rehabilitation or adaptation of historic structures.

Financial regulation agencies and authorities—that older buildings and neighborhoods will not be redlined.

Environmental impact statements—that these submissions include preservation review requirements.

Federal Community Development Block Grant Program—that preservation may be assisted by the program.

Rehabilitation assistance programs—that guidelines for sensitive rehabilitation of historic properties are available to those implementing or participating in the program.

QUESTIONS TO BE CONSIDERED

Is increased private sector participation in the development of public regulations desirable? What steps, if any, should be taken to alter the present state of private sector participation? What regulation areas need new or increased attention from preservationists? Is there a need for a monitoring and information service about regulation matters? What special considerations come into play in the case of regulations at national, state and local levels but in different ways and varyingly and voluntarily adopted? How does the impact of private preservation organization participation in the regulation process differ from that of participation by other public agencies or regulatory entities?

LOCAL PRESERVATION LEGISLATIVE AGENDAS

The June 1978 U.S. Supreme Court decision on Grand Central Terminal supports the validity of laws creating landmarks and historic district commissions throughout the United States. The Court upheld the preservation of a landmark whose owner wanted to destroy portions of it and also set a standard for rejecting demolition requests when a landmark is being put to a reasonable beneficial use. Most of the municipal preservation ordinances that have been passed in nearly 500 communities do not go as far as the opinion of the Court would allow. It will take time and effort to change them. There may be strong political opposition locally to taking advantage of the powers possible under the decision. It should be noted that the case also calls for procedures that may be more complicated than those of present ordinances.

The private sector also will be examining how preservation relates to local efforts to revitalize cities and to rehabilitate neighborhoods. Some persons reject using preservation to help neighborhoods while others want preservation activities to be extended to areas that do not qualify as historic districts. There is increased concern about the guidelines and standards under which local laws are administered; critics believe that preservationists reach too many ad hoc decisions. State legislatures are reviewing the scope of the programs run by state historic preservation offices and at the same time are considering how much power should be given to municipalities that start local programs. As preservation grows, state laws and regulations may restrict a city's program in response to pressure from owners and government departments. Finally, government must decide how strictly it wants to regulate property it owns and funds that may affect historic property.

QUESTIONS TO BE CONSIDERED

How strong does the private sector want local preservation ordinances to be? Is there good community support for prohibiting the demolition of historic buildings that can be put to a "reasonable beneficial use"? What should the private sector do to protect historic buildings in areas and communities where there is no local legislation? How strict a standard does the private sector expect to be enforced in the regulation of alterations to designated property? May a local landmarks commission be established as an independent government agency or must it be created as a part of a larger department? Will its powers only be advisory? What is the role of the private sector and what is the responsibility of government in saving a building threatened with demolition?

NATIONAL PRESERVATION LEGISLATIVE AGENDA

The federal government historically has taken the initiative in identifying and protecting the nation's cultural resources. In the 19th century, the federal government first acted to protect specific sites, including Yellowstone Park, the first national park, and the Civil War battlefields.

In 1906, Congress enacted its first general preservation measure, the Antiquities Act, which authorized the president to designate as national monuments "historic landmarks, historic and prehistoric structures and other objects of historic or scientific interest" situated on federal lands. The Antiquities Act retains a requirement of national significance for the application of federal protection, and that protection was primarily federal ownership. There are no protections for similar sites on private property and no check on federal actions that might harm culturally significant properties. The act did, however, break with the tradition of separate Congressional actions and provided an administrative mechanism for determination of the significance of cultural properties.

The Historic Sites Act of 1935 established a national policy of cultural preservation and provided the authority for the development of an administrative program to identify and evaluate cultural resources of national significance. Significantly, for the first time, the federal government was to consider that preservation policy in the implementation of federal plans and programs. Subject to Congressional appropriations, the Secretary of the Interior was authorized to enter into agreements with state and local governments and with private individuals and organizations to preserve properties and to acquire them.

In recognition of the accelerating loss of significant resources and of the limited abilities of the federal government, Congress chartered the private National Trust for Historic Preservation in 1949 to further the federal historic preservation policy and to facilitate public participation in preservation efforts.

To meet the shortcomings of previous federal legislation and to stimulate the preservation of properties in nonfederal ownership, the National Historic Preservation Act of 1966 established a program of grants-in-aid to the states for the identification and preservation of properties of state and local significance, as well as those of national significance, and grants-in-aid to the National Trust to carry out its responsibilities. It created a mechanism for review by the Advisory Council on Historic Preservation of federal actions that might affect properties in the National Register of Historic Places. In 1976, the Advisory Council was made an independent federal agency and a National Historic Preservation Fund was authorized through 1981.

In the Tax Reform Act of 1976, the Internal Revenue Code was amended to provide through 1981 incentives to the private sector for the rehabilitation (as approved by the Secretary of the Interior) of historic income-producing structures and to provide disincentives for their destruction. The Tax Reform Act, in addition, provided taxpayers a charitable deduction against income for the donation of partial interests in property such as easements for conservation purposes.

Recent federal legislation with primary purposes other than preservation has also benefited preservation. Examples are the U.S. Department of Housing and Urban Development's Community Development Block Grant program, the U.S. Department of Commerce's public works programs and environmental reviews pursuant to the National Environmental Policy Act of 1969.

President Carter has called for a comprehensive federal program to identify, acquire and protect the nation's natural

237

and historic heritage, a National Heritage Policy Act. The act proposes to: (a) extend the authorization of the National Historic Preservation Fund; (b) codify federal agency responsibilities to identify and protect historic resources; (c) protect nationally significant properties from adverse federal actions unless there is no feasible or prudent alternative; and (d) expand the National Register to include networks, cultural landscapes and neighborhoods.

Congressional committees will be conducting oversight investigations of the federal preservation program. At issue, in part, is the extension of the authorizations for the National Historic Preservation Fund and for the preservation tax provisions.

QUESTIONS TO BE CONSIDERED

Do federal tax disincentives to the demolition of historically significant structures and to their replacement with new structures conflict with other federal, state and local programs to stimulate urban redevelopment? Will opposition to the tax disincentives undermine nominations to the National Register of Historic Places? Are direct government subsidies for the preservation of historic resources more effective or more appropriate than indirect subsidies provided by the tax laws? Should private preservation organizations accelerate formal efforts to influence legislation? Are national legislators being made aware of and a part of preservation efforts at home? Is it in the interest of preservation to organize support, through political action committees, for pro-preservation candidates for Congress? Will the juxtaposition of federal programs for the protection of both natural and cultural resources adversely affect the federal and state programs directed to cultural resources? Are additional, substantive measures, such as the "no feasible or prudent alternative" standard, needed to protect nationally or less significant resources from federal government actions?

WILLIAMSBURG CONFERENCE PARTICIPANTS

Abel, Betts, project manager, Oliver T. Carr Company, Washington, D.C.

Abell, Helen, Louisville, Ky.; vice chairman, Board of Trustees, National Trust.

Adler, Leopold, II, president, Savannah Landmark Rehabilitation Project, Savannah, Ga.; member, Board of Trustees, National Trust.

Baker, William A., naval architect, Hingham, Mass.

Baldridge, Joan Williams, state historic preservation officer, Little Rock, Ark.

Berkebile, Robert, Patty Berkebile Nelson Associates, Kansas City, Mo.

Berner, Robert, executive director, Foundation for San Francisco's Architectural Heritage, San Francisco, Calif.

Bickel, Minnette C., executive director, Georgia Trust for Historic Preservation, Atlanta, Ga.

Black, Charles M., ASID, Honolulu, Hawaii; member, Board of Trustees, National Trust.

Boasberg, Tersh, Boasberg, Hewes, Finkelstein & Klores, Washington, D.C.

Briggs, Porter, editor and publisher, *American Preservation*, Little Rock, Ark.

Brink, Peter H., executive director, Galveston Historical Foundation, Galveston, Tex.

Brown, R. Michael, ASID, New York, N.Y.; national chairman for historic preservation, American Society of Interior Designers.

Byard, Paul S., New York, N.Y.; president, National Center for Preservation Law.

Candee, Richard M., Kittery, Me.; preservation consultant, Boston University.

Carter, Calvin, Tampa, Fla.; member, Advisory Council on Historic Preservation.

Cecil, William A. V., president, Biltmore House and Gardens, Asheville, N.C.; chairman, Historic House Association of America.

Chapman, Bruce, secretary of state, Olympia, Wash.; member, Board of Trustees, National Trust.

Churchill, Stephanie, executive director, Utah Heritage Foundation, Salt Lake City, Utah.

Clark, Carol, assistant director, New York Landmarks Conservancy, New York, N.Y.

Collins, Robertson E., Medford, Ore.; conference chairman; vice chairman, Board of Trustees, National Trust.

Conaway, Franklin P., urban affairs consultant, Brewer & Brewer Sons, Chillicothe, Ohio.

Costonis, Prof. John J., School of Law, New York University, New York, N.Y.

Gayle, Margot, president, Friends of Cast-Iron Architecture, New York, N.Y.

Giebner, Prof. Robert C., Department of Architecture, University of Arizona, Tucson, Ariz.; member, Board of Trustees, National Trust.

Graham, Roy E., Williamsburg, Va.; vice president, Association for Preservation Technology.

Gualtieri, Mardi, mayor, Los Gatos, Calif.

Halsey, Stephen S., vice president, American Express Foundation, New York, N.Y.

Hansel, John E., special assistant for the environment, Economic Development Administration, U. S. Department of Commerce, Washington, D.C.

Harrington, Billie, executive director, Landmark Society of Western New York, Rochester, N.Y.

Harrison, B. Powell, Leesburg, Va.; member, Board of Advisors, National Trust.

Hart, William B., Jr., executive director, New Hampshire Charitable Fund, Concord, N.H.

Heath, Annabelle, vice president for urban activities, Federal National Mortgage Association, Washington, D.C.

Holmes, Nancy H., Mobile, Ala.; chairman, Board of Advisors, National Trust.

Hosmer, Prof. Charles B., Jr., Principia College, Elsah, Ill.

Howard, J. Myrick, executive director, Historic Preservation Fund of North Carolina, Raleigh, N.C.

Huhta, James K., Murfreesboro, Tenn.; chairman, National Council for Preservation Education.

Humelsine, Carlisle H., Williamsburg, Va.; chairman, Board of Trustees, National Trust.

Jahns, Jeffrey, chairman, Program and Policy Committee, Landmarks Preservation Council, Chicago, Ill.

Johnston, Douglas A., assistant attorney general, State of North Carolina, Raleigh, N.C.

Kane, Thomas J., Pleasantville, N.Y.; chairman, Committee for Historic Preservation, American Society of Landscape Architects.

Knight, Roy F., assistant director, Architecture, Planning and Design, National Endowment for the Arts, Washington, D.C.

Knott, Lawson B., Jr., Arlington, Va.; member, Board of Trustees, National Trust.

Liebs, Chester H., director, Historic Preservation Program, University of Vermont, Burlington, Vt.

Linker, Wayne A., executive director, Connecticut Trust for Historic Preservation, New Haven, Conn.

Longsworth, Nellie L., president, Preservation Action, Washington, D.C.

Lowell, James W., executive director, Neighborhood Housing Services, Inc., Anacostia, Washington, D.C.

Lu, Weiming, director of urban design, Lowertown Redevelopment Corporation, St. Paul, Minn.

Lynch, Robert P., Warren, R.I.; chairman, Rhode Island Chapter, Preservation Action.

McGimsey, Charles R., III, director, Arkansas Archeological Survey, University of Arkansas Museum, Fayetteville, Ark.

MacDougall, Elisabeth, director, Studies in the History of Landscape Architecture, Dumbarton Oaks, Washington, D.C.

Merritt, Louise McAllister, director, Historic Albany Foundation, Albany, N.Y.

Middleton, Michael, executive director, Civic Trust, London, England.

Morton, W. Brown, III, Waterford, Va.; chairman, United States Committee, International Council of Monuments and Sites.

Murtagh, William J., keeper, National Register of Historic Places, Heritage Conservation and Recreation Service, U. S. Department of the Interior, Washington, D.C.

Myers, Hyman, AIA, restoration architect, Day & Zimmerman Associates, Merion, Pa.

Orenstein, Kenneth, coordinator, Downtown Development and Preservation Team, Mayor's Office of Community Development, Providence, R.I.

Orr, Gordon D., Jr., AIA, campus architect, University Planning and Construction, University of Wisconsin, Madison, Wis.

Owens, Christopher, executive director, Old Town Restorations, St. Paul, Minn.

Park, Jeffrey J., secretary, Corporate Responsibility Investment Committee, AETNA Life and Casualty Insurance Company, Hartford, Conn.

Pearce, John, director, Graduate Program in Historic Preservation, The George Washington University, Washington, D.C.

Puckett, Robert A., director, Historic Wichita, Wichita, Kans.

Reece, Beverly, Federal National Mortgage Association, Washington, D.C.

Reilly, William K., president, The Conservation Foundation, Washington, D.C.

Reynolds, Anthony, MAI, Reynolds & Reynolds, Inc., Washington, D.C.

Reynolds, Judith, MAI, Reynolds & Reynolds, Inc., Washington, D.C.

Rogers, Jerry L., chief, Office of Archeology and Historic Preservation, Heritage Conservation and Recreation Service, U.S. Department of the Interior, Washington, D.C.

Rushing, Byron, Museum of Afro-American History/Roxbury Historical Society, Boston, Mass.

Russ, Joel B., executive director, Greater Portland Landmarks, Portland, Me.

Satrom, Joseph A., Bismarck, N.D.; member, Board of Advisors, National Trust.

Schluntz, Roger L., AIA, Association of Collegiate Schools of Architecture, Washington, D.C.

Short, James R., director, preservation and research, Colonial Williamsburg Foundation, Williamsburg, Va.

Smith, Ann Webster, deputy to the secretary-general, International Council of Monuments and Sites, Paris, France.

Sower, John, director, National Development Council, Washington, D.C.

Spink, Frank H., Jr., director of publications, Urban Land Institute, Washington, D.C.

Stipe, Prof. Robert E., School of Design, North Carolina State University, Raleigh; member, Board of Trustees, National Trust.

Thorman, Jan, Heritage Conservation and Recreation Service, U. S. Department of the Interior, Washington, D.C.

Townsend, Arthur C., state historic preservation officer, Denver, Colo.

Trementozzi, Miriam, preservation consultant, Burlington, Vt.

True, Conrad, administrative director, San Antonio Conservation Society, San Antonio, Tex.

Utley, Beatrice, Hampton, Conn.; chairman, National Museum House Committee, National Society of Colonial Dames of America.

Waite, Diana S., executive director, Preservation League of New York State, Albany, N.Y.

Webb, Roger W., president, Architectural Heritage Foundation, Boston, Mass.

Weiss, Prof. Norman R., Historic Preservation Program, Columbia University, New York, N.Y.

Wellington, Margot, executive director, Municipal Art Society, New York, N.Y.

Westmoreland, Carl B., executive director, Madisonville Housing Services, Cincinnati, Ohio; member, Board of Trustees, National Trust.

Whyte, William H., Jr., director, Street Life Project, New York, N.Y.

Williamson, Frederick C., director, Rhode Island Department of Community Affairs, Providence, R.I.

Williamson, J. Reid, executive director, Historic Landmarks Foundation of Indiana, Indianapolis, Ind.

Wilkinson, William D., director, Mariners Museum, Newport News, Va.

Winkeller, Paul, assistant to the administrator for historic preservation, U.S. General Services Administration, Washington, D.C.

Wood, Anthony C., legislative and administrative aide, New York City Council, New York, N.Y.

Wright, Anne St. Clair, chairman, Board of Trustees, Historic Annapolis, Annapolis, Md.

Wright, Russell, AIA, Warren, R.I.

Yip, Christopher, architectural historian, Chinatown Neighborhood Improvement Resource Center, San Francisco, Calif.

Ziegler, Arthur P., Jr., president, Pittsburgh History and Landmarks Foundation, Pittsburgh, Pa.; member, Board of Trustees, National Trust.

OTHER PRESERVATION PRESS BOOKS

America's Forgotten Architecture. National Trust for Historic Preservation, Tony P. Wrenn, Elizabeth D. Mulloy. The best overview of preservation today. Surveys in 475 photos what is worth saving and how to do it. 312 pages, illustrated, bibliography, appendixes. Published by Pantheon Books. $20 hardbound, $8.95 paperbound.

Built to Last: A Handbook on Recycling Old Buildings. Gene Bunnell, Massachusetts Department of Community Affairs. Facts and figures on several dozen adaptive use projects, detailing how and why these buildings were saved. 126 pages, illustrated, bibliography. $6.95 paperbound.

Directory of Private, Nonprofit Preservation Organizations: State and Local Levels. National Trust for Historic Preservation. The first guide to more than 4,000 local preservation organizations, neighborhood associations, landmarks and historic district commissions, statewide organizations, historical societies and allied groups. 136 pages. $6.95 paperbound.

Economic Benefits of Preserving Old Buildings. Shows how recycling saves money, with examples of projects large and small, public and private. Contributors include architects, preservationists, developers and public officials. 168 pages, illustrated. $7.95 paperbound.

The Failure to Preserve the Queen City Hotel, Cumberland, Md. Dianne Newell. Case Studies in Preservation 1. Examines the struggle and failure to save an endangered landmark. 36 pages, illustrated, appendixes. $4.50 paperbound.

A Grand Strategy: The Scenario for Saving the Grand Opera House, Wilmington, Del. Robert Stoddard. Case Studies in Preservation 3. Analyzes the community preservation effort and fund-raising strategy that saved a Victorian theater for continued use. 44 pages, illustrated, appendixes. $4.50 paperbound.

246

A Guide to Federal Programs for Historic Preservation, 1976 Supplement. Nancy D. Schultz, ed. A guide to finding preservation funding in the federal government. Some 200 programs of 49 agencies are indexed. 110 pages. $4.95 paperbound.

The History of the National Trust for Historic Preservation, 1963-1973. Elizabeth D. Mulloy. A record both of the National Trust and of the preservation movement's rise nationally during the 1960s. Appendixes present valuable reference material. 315 pages, color illustrated, appendixes. $9.95 hardbound.

Information: A Preservation Sourcebook. A compendium of two dozen publications from the National Trust "Information" series. Topics range from basic preservation procedures and rehabilitating old houses to public and private financing, revolving funds, economic benefits of preservation, neighborhoods and special building types. Annually updated for permanent reference. 400 pages, illustrated, bibliography. $15 binder.

The Making of a Historic District, Swiss Avenue, Dallas, Tex. Lyn Dunsavage and Virginia Talkington. Case Studies in Preservation 2. Documents the emergence and success of a local preservation group, emphasizing the role of communications in obtaining historic district status. 40 pages, illustrated, appendixes. $4.50 paperbound.

Monumentum. Terry B. Morton, ed. Leading preservationists view the past, present and future of preservation in the United States, providing a concise introduction to preservation and its current concerns. 128 pages, illustrated. $10 paperbound.

Old and New Architecture: Design Relationship. A provocative exploration by 18 prominent architects and preservationists of how to design new buildings and additions next to old ones. Topics include design theory, historic district protection, architectural controls, design guidelines, review boards and adaptive use. 280 pages, illustrated, bibliography, index. $25 hardbound.

Presence of the Past: A History of the Preservation Movement in the United States before Williamsburg. Charles B. Hosmer, Jr. A thorough account of the movement's inception and landmark achievements. Published by G.P. Putnam's Sons. 386 pages, illustrated, bibliography. $12.95 hardbound.

Preservation and Conservation: Principles and Practices. An in-depth examination of the technical aspects of restoration and object conservation, from preservation philosophy and education to restoration materials, techniques and maintenance, with case studies. 547 pages, illustrated, bibliography. $17.95 hardbound.

Tax Incentives for Historic Preservation. Gregory E. Andrews, ed. The Tax Reform Act of 1976 and the Revenue Act of 1978 provide federal tax incentives for preservation that are examined in this book, together with other benefits available in numerous states and cities. The book's contributors are leading preservationists and attorneys. 232 pages, case studies, appendixes. $12.95 paperbound.

What Style Is It? John Poppeliers, S. Allen Chambers, Nancy B. Schwartz. One of the most popular concise guides to American architectural styles, prepared by staff of the Historic American Buildings Survey. 48 pages, illustrated, glossary, bibliography. $4.95 paperbound.

To order Preservation Press books, send total of book prices (less 10 percent discount for National Trust members), plus $1.50 postage and handling, to: Preservation Bookshop, 1600 H Street, N.W., Washington, D.C. 20006. Residents of California, Massachusetts, New York and South Carolina please add applicable sales tax. Make checks payable to the National Trust and allow at least three weeks for delivery. A complete list of publications is available by writing:

THE PRESERVATION PRESS
National Trust for Historic Preservation
1785 Massachusetts Avenue, N.W., Washington, D.C. 20036